the series on school refo

Patricia A. Wasley
Bank Street College of Education

Ann Lieberman
NCREST

J

New York University

SERIES EDITORS

This series also incorporates earlier titles in the Professional Development and Practice Series

School Reform Behind the Scenes

Joseph P. McDonald
Thomas Hatch
Edward Kirby
Nancy Ames
Norris M. Haynes
Edward T. Joyner

AFTERWORD BY

Janet Whitla
James Comer
Howard Gardner
Theodore Sizer

TEACHERS COLLEGE PRESS

Teachers College
Columbia University
New York and London

Published by Teachers College Press, 1234 Amsterdam Avenue, New York, NY 10027

Library of Congress Cataloging-in-Publication Data

School reform behind the scenes / Joseph P. McDonald . . . [et al.].
    p.   cm. — (The series on school reform)
   Includes bibliographical references and index.
   ISBN 0-8077-3861-1 (cloth). — ISBN 0-8077-3926-X (pbk.)
   1. School improvement programs—United States—Case studies.
2. Community and school—United States—Case studies. 3. College
—school cooperation—United States—Case studies. 4. Educational
change—United States—Case studies. I. McDonald, Joseph P.
II. Series.
LB2822.82.S368 1999
306.43'2—dc21   99-17328

ISBN 0-8077-3926-X (paper)
ISBN 0-8077-3861-1 (cloth)

Printed on acid-free paper

Manufactured in the United States of America

06 05 04 03 02 01 00 99   8 7 6 5 4 3 2 1

Contents

Acknowledgments

The development of this book and the work of the ATLAS Seminar were supported by the generous contributions of the Spencer Foundation, the John D. and Catherine T. MacArthur Foundation, and the Rockefeller Foundation. In addition to acknowledging the generous support of the foundations that funded the ATLAS Seminar, the authors also wish to acknowledge the support of the Annenberg Institute for School Reform at Brown University and The Carnegie Foundation for the Advancement of Teaching which funded some writing and editing time for Joseph McDonald and Edward Kirby and for Thomas Hatch, respectively. We would like to thank all the members of the Seminar and, in particular, members of the four partner organizations and ATLAS who participated in the development, discussion, and review of this work. We would also like to thank Carrie Peterson, Sara Lightner, and Ruby Kerawalla for their invaluable assistance in the preparation of the manuscript. The authors are solely responsible for the content presented here.

One Hundred Years of School Reform

In the second-to-the-last decade of the twentieth century, the United States began a long and laborious effort to reform its schools. The most obvious motivation was economic: to secure for the twenty-first century an American work force educated well enough to compete against a united Europe and economic forces in Asia. But an older motivation also tagged along, namely, to deliver at last on the American promise of equitable opportunity for all Americans. For once, economic interests and democratic ones seemed compatible.

From a distance, this remarkable effort seems largely a project of government, or of an alliance between government and American business. So, for example, its opening scene often is taken to be the one where a commission appointed by President Reagan declared baldly, "If an unfriendly foreign power had attempted to impose on America the mediocre educational performance that exists today, we might well have viewed it as an act of war" (National Commission on Excellence in Education, 1983, p. 5). Another dramatic scene was when President Bush and the 50 governors, threatening the historical precedent of local educational policy making in the United States, met in Charlottesville, Virginia, to adopt a set of common "National Goals" to direct reform. Still another was when President Clinton and the Congress produced Goals 2000, legislation that among other things financed the development of a voluntary set of national curriculum standards. And still another dramatic scene was when the 50 governors met the CEOs of many American corporations at a "summit" on school reform that called for new and tougher standards of accountability in education. Linking these and other scenes across little more than 10 years, were efforts by nearly every state to enact school reform legislation and otherwise change state-level school policy, often spurred by business interests.

Some of the effects of these various efforts have threatened long-established habits of schooling and century-old power arrangements. By the last years of the twentieth century, the whole country seemed awash in school policy experimentation involving new curriculum standards, new testing regimens, governance changes, school reconstitution, charter schools, voucher and school privatization schemes, and more.

Behind the dramatic scenes, however, lies another school reform story. This is the one in which numerous independent organizations have worked steadily on school reform within and among the schools themselves. Their colorful names evoke a range of ideologies and approaches: Paideia, Foxfire, the New Standards Project, Accelerated Schools, the League of Professional Schools, Success for All, and others. Many, although not all, are associated with universities. In most cases, however, the association is a marginal one, dependent on what is called "soft" funding. Such funding sometimes has come from government, either directly or indirectly, and often from corporate donors like Exxon, IBM, Citibank, and others, both large and small. But the greatest source of funding for independent, behind-the-scenes work in school reform has been foundations—both regional ones and also national ones like the John D. and Catherine T. MacArthur Foundation, the Rockefeller Foundation, the Pew Charitable Trusts, the Carnegie Corporation, and the DeWitt Wallace Reader's Digest Fund.

The efforts of the independent school reform organizations have complemented the governmental efforts in many respects, giving them the reach they otherwise lacked. Sometimes, though, the independent organizations have worked to blunt government efforts when the latter seemed insensitive to the realities of life in schools. But whether supporting front-of-the-curtain work or not, these behind-the-scenes independent efforts have considerable experience of school change. Through trial and error, research and reflection, the activists at the heart of these efforts have gained much knowledge of how schools change and of what real change looks like and feels like within the communities of the schools themselves. Therefore, their work behind the scenes also might be said to be work within what researchers call the black box—the thing that lies between inputs and outcomes and makes the two somehow connect.

Within the black box, the terms of the struggle for reform have been somewhat different than they have seemed outside: no rhetoric about educational mediocrity and acts of war, and, naturally, far less reliance than among government efforts on the use of incentives and sanctions. Here, in Seymour Sarason's (1982, 1996) elegant phrase, the culture of the school and the problem of change have been more salient.

This book goes behind the scenes of late-twentieth-century American school reform to focus closely on the work of five independent school reform organizations and to explore what they do and what they know. The five include two of the largest national school reform networks: James Comer's School Development Program at Yale University and Theodore

Sizer's Coalition of Essential Schools. They also include one of the oldest and most influential research and development efforts in American education, Education Development Center, led by Janet Whitla, and an influential research program at Harvard University called Project Zero, coled by Howard Gardner and David Perkins. Finally, they include a fifth organization that the other four created jointly at the invitation of the New American Schools Development Corporation (NASDC), itself an independent school reform organization.[1] In 1990, NASDC funded an effort by the four to pool their expertise in order to create (in NASDC's language) a "break the mold" school design for the twenty-first century American school. The new partners called this effort ATLAS Communities, or simply ATLAS (for Authentic Teaching and Learning for All Students).

The expertise represented in the ATLAS partnership reflects 100 years of school reform. That is, adding the number of years that the four partner organizations have been active in trying to achieve reform of American schooling yields 100 years of experience, struggle, frustration, and intermittent success—and also 100 years of accumulated knowledge of a certain craft. Some people call it the craft of the "change agent," but we avoid the term in this book because to us it implies exclusive agency, as if the people who work in schools and the parents whose children attend them were not also crucial to change. The craft we speak of is more about trying to arrange things so as to empower and support inside agents. This is difficult work in and of itself, but it is made more difficult by the fact that few who have ever done it well have left a record of what they did. As a result, others working behind the scenes have long had a tendency to start new initiatives from scratch, to ignore the work of others who have gone before. Moreover, those working in front of the curtain—especially policy makers—are apt to think that their reforms are the first serious ones. A consequence of both these circumstances, as Seymour Sarason (1982, 1991, 1996) points out, is a continuing proliferation of Type A reforms and very few Type B reforms (those that build on the successes of earlier efforts and respond to their failures).

The reform called ATLAS was conceived as a Type B reform, an effort to create a new initiative out of 100 years of diverse reform experience. Its designers anticipated bringing together the most productive and successful ideas and practices of the four partner organizations. Yet, as we will recount below and in Chapter 6, the designers were unprepared for all the learning that a second-generation reform requires. They were enormously burdened as well by an expectation—largely imposed on them— that what is needed in second-generation reform is not the wisdom of collective experience, well reflected on, but rather its integration into a grand design. Luckily, as a result of the generosity of the Spencer Foundation, and John D. and Catherine T. MacArthur Foundation, and the Rockefeller Foundation, the partners found time to do more than design collaboratively. They found time to think together and write together as members of what was called the ATLAS Seminar, and in the process to reflect on their own experience in ATLAS and before ATLAS. One outcome of this effort is the account of their organizations' theories of action and of their own craft knowledge that constitutes this book.

The book is intended for all who work for school change in this unusually sustained era of school reform in the United States. It is written for other people, like the authors who work on activist research or in reform-based networks, and who provide professional development and school development opportunities for educators. It is written for educators themselves who are working for change inside schools—as far behind the scenes as one can go. Nearly every conception of change we explore here, and every tactic we mention, is serviceable there. It is written for change-minded policy makers at all levels of the complex system of American schooling, who must understand the complexity with which they contend in order to have any hope of affecting it. Finally, it is written for still other citizens who are worried about the state of the schools at the turn of the century and who would like to know what it might take to ensure that American public schooling survives. We think what we portray of a hundred collective years of change efforts offers not only a practical guide to school reform but a faithful, realistic, and hopeful account of its dynamics.

On the other hand, this book does not provide an exhaustive account of the work of the ATLAS organizations. To prepare such an account, we would have had to take our research much farther than the ATLAS Seminar, and especially into the schools where the ATLAS partners have worked. If we had been able to manage such a project, this would be a book full of the voices of teachers and of children. Instead, it is full of the voices of people who work *with* schools rather than *in* them. At times, it may strike the reader, therefore, as somewhat removed from the heart of the matter. One early reviewer, warning us that this might be so, wrote, "Reformers tend to think they are the center of the action because they are the center of their own action." We admit that in the pages that follow—and for the reasons explained above—we focus on our own action. We acknowledge, however, that our action, like the action of other reformers even farther from school than ourselves—in governors' mansions, mayoral offices, legislatures, and board rooms—is only as good as its impact on teaching and learning in school. School is the real center of action.

To learn about the impact of the ATLAS partners on teaching and learning in the schools they work with, we invite readers to explore what we and others have written elsewhere about this important topic. To this end, we have included an appendix, which contains a special reading list, as well as information about sources of other information regarding the work of the School Development Program, the Coalition of Essential Schools, Education Development Center, Project Zero, and the ATLAS Project.

THE ATLAS CHALLENGE

When the ATLAS collaborators began their collaboration, they were full of hope about what they might do together. However, they did not at first give much thought to what they might learn from each other in order to create a successful second-generation reform. Whenever they had occasion in those days to catalogue the differences in what they knew, they tended to account for these differences solely in terms of content knowledge. Thus Education Development Center (EDC) knew a lot about curriculum and technology; the School Development Program (SDP) knew elementary schools particularly well; the Coalition of Essential Schools (CES) knew how high schools work and change; Project Zero (PZ) knew about performance assessment and its potential for improving classroom practice, and so on. They tended not to focus on their approaches to change or on the assumptions that underlie these approaches. Meanwhile, as they were to discover, working very hard side by side does not by itself ensure that craft knowledge will be shared or assumptions uncovered. In this case, the differences (and similarities) in what the ATLAS collaborators knew about the work of fostering serious school change tended to remain submerged in the ways they interacted, in the problems and issues they sought to pursue, and in the choices they made as they worked. Often, this submergence caused trouble: It was not always easy to coordinate efforts or to come to consensus about what to do. When they first began to address the problem, however, the resulting presentations about each organization's missions and methods, while helpful, tended to leave out critical information. Missing in particular was information about beliefs and practices so basic to each organization as to seem to its members hardly necessary to explain—especially to colleagues also involved in behind-the-scenes efforts at school reform. At one of the last gatherings of the ATLAS Seminar, Tom Hatch of Project Zero reflected on one of his first meetings with members of the Coalition of Essential Schools.

> I went to the Coalition of Essential Schools to discuss plans for the ATLAS Seminar. I went expecting to talk about the key issues we should pursue in a series of monthly meetings. Instead, the conver-

sation focused on who the participants would be and the extent to which practitioners would be involved. I kept trying to steer the conversation back to the "issues." In my mind, if we could identify some of the issues and needs that had emerged in the work of the four organizations, we could then look for the appropriate people to explore them. I was conditioned to think of the seminar in this way because I come from a research organization, one that tries to make change happen by elucidating the right issues in the right ways.

It was not until a year later that I really understood the CES staff members' concerns. By then I had noticed that almost no meeting at CES takes place without practitioners present. CES meetings regularly include teachers and administrators who have left their schools for the day, who are on sabbatical, or who have recently joined the CES staff. The focus of the CES work is less on issues than the life of schools and classrooms, and the work is predicated on the idea that the issues and the stimulus for change should come from the practitioners themselves. From that perspective, determining who the participants of our seminar were going to be *was* the issue.

What Hatch bumped up against that day, and what he acknowledges took him a year to understand, was that there was a different theory at work within CES than the one he was most used to. Ultimately, the challenge in ATLAS was to understand and ultimately to deal with such differences in theory. We mean the word *theory* here in the broadest sense, as applying not only to activists' explicit rationales for doing whatever they do, but also to the sometimes tacit assumptions that underlie them. In fact, different craft knowledge of school change had accumulated within the four ATLAS organizations over a collective span of reform work roughly 100 years long, and ATLAS work necessarily would involve negotiating the differences. The ATLAS collaborators tried to do this on the fly as they worked together, but on-the-fly negotiation proved insufficient. What ATLAS clearly needed was an opportunity to reflect on what its partners knew. Eventually, such an opportunity was provided by the grant that funded the ATLAS Seminar. The Seminar ran for 4 years and included among its members all the authors of this book.[2]

The book presents what we learned from a series of long and intimate interviews of senior staff members from each organization that we conducted as part of the ATLAS Seminar, and from special Seminar sessions that we held in the staff rooms of each organization. We first analyzed the interviews by means of a simple structure. The reader may wish to keep this structure in mind since it is embedded in the design of the chapters that follow. It is based on the idea that behind-the-scenes work for school change involves the application of principles, strategies, and moves. Each is associated with a different level of organizational influence and personal preference.

Principles are tied to organizational histories and emphases, and reflect key organizational commitments. Many principles are highly explicit in the discourse of the organizations, although others—including some crucial to the definition of desirable change—are rather understated. Our expectation—given the strong cultures and missions of these organizations, as well as their age—was that at the level of principles we would find little inconsistency *within* each organization, although quite a bit *across* them. In fact, we found significant amounts of inconsistency with respect to principles both across and within the organizations. However, we learned to associate the latter with the resiliency of the organizations across 10 to 30 years of continually shifting contexts for reform. In the end, we decided to refer to this phenomenon as internal paradox rather than internal inconsistency, and to regard it as a source of strength.

We defined *strategies* as particular designs for taking action. We expected to find that these shift from time to time within organizations, the changes arising from different opportunities and constraints, and we expected to find multiple strategies at work within each organization. Indeed, we thought we might find almost as much strategic variation within as across the ATLAS partners, and we did.

Finally, we defined *moves*, the third element of our preliminary analytical structure, as the product of an intersection of principles and particular strategies with the personal experiences of individual reformers. We joked that we chose the term so as to compare ourselves with basketball players, but we realized at the same time that the joke had its serious side. In fact, experienced reformers who are used to the complicated contexts of actual schools work from the gut as well as the head, and have an overlearned repertoire. By asking our colleagues to reflect on their repertoire of "moves," we hoped that our research might make available for wider use some ways of working for change that tend to reside only in the tacit understanding of experienced practitioners.

This analytical structure involving principles, strategies, and moves proved quite serviceable in most respects. It helped us organize our collection of data—beginning empirically with staff members' own words about their moves. And it helped us begin our analysis of these data—inferring from the moves the strategies and principles. It gave us only momentary pause that we needed much more than inference to uncover strategies and principles, that we also needed another round of interviews and a lot of documentary data too. Later, however, when we ran into some trouble analyzing our data, we started to realize that we needed a sharper analytical structure than the simple one we had invented.

The problem with the original one was that it lacked power to explain the dynamism in our data. This dynamism was more evident at first in the data on ATLAS itself, since—being new—ATLAS revealed its turbulence more readily; but it was present as well in our data on the four ATLAS partners. The other problem with the structure of principle–strategy–moves was that it assumed too much causality in the links—as if moves were wholly derivative of strategies, for example, or as if principles could wholly predict strategic choices. In thinking first about ATLAS itself, and then about the four partners again, we realized that this assumption was unwarranted.

Searching for a sharper analytical structure, we found one in Donald Schön's work. The reader may recall that in our analysis of Tom Hatch's anecdote above—the one about bumping into what seemed to him the mysterious CES habit of inviting school people to meetings—we said that he had bumped into a different *theory* than the one he was used to. Our use of the word in this context owes much to Donald Schön's work. He argues that activist organizations like the ones we studied may be said to "hold" a theory of action (Argyris & Schön, 1974/1992; Schön, 1997; Schön & McDonald, 1998). A theory of action is a complex and layered organizational phenomenon. First, Schön says, there is the organization's *espoused theory*. Expression of this may be found in mission statements, brochures, speeches, and the like. It also may surface more or less explicitly at crucial moments: in hiring or terminating key personnel, in coping with sudden crises, or at strategic watersheds. Espoused theories are not necessarily coherent, however (Argyris & Schön, 1974/1992; Schön, 1997). In particular, those constructed by coalitions—ones like the ATLAS partnership or, indeed, the ATLAS partners themselves (each being a kind of coalition of theoretical and practical interests)—may contain unexamined or unacknowledged inconsistencies. These are associated with different assumptions that different parties bring to bear. The inconsistencies may represent, as we suggest above, a kind of cache of resiliency, or they may represent trouble waiting to happen.

Whether coherent or not, espoused theory must be enacted into designs. These are the materials, technologies, structures, and strategies that an organization invents as it pursues some initiative. In the enacting of designs, still more theory comes into play. That is partly because new people with different assumptions may be involved in the designing—this is nearly always the case in most reform organizations, given their characteristic staff turnover. It also may be because the designs somehow distort original intentions, and for all practical purposes introduce different and even contradictory ones. Thus what Schön calls *design theory*—or the theory that seems implicit in designs—may be more or less congruent with espoused theory. It also may be more or less coherent. Particularly where the tasks are complex, as in school reform, one must expect some degree of incoherence across an initiative's strategies. Again, this can be a source of resilience—although it also can be a source of organizational conflict (Schön & McDonald, 1998).

Finally, the third layer or facet of an overall theory of action is what Schön calls *theory in use*. This is the theory implicit in what actually happens on the ground as an activist organization goes to work or an initiative takes hold. The best way to think about the theory in use of organizations like the ATLAS partners is to consider it from the perspective of the schools that actually use their processes, principles, theories, and programs. From such a perspective, one can expect to see a degree of distortion—sometimes minimal, sometimes serious. There are many sources of such distortion: local circumstances, the incorporation of another whole set of assumptions, misinterpretation or deliberate misappropriation of ideas or designs, and (not insignificantly) learning from experience. One mark of a successful reform organization is the extent to which it notices and reflects on distortion, what it learns from it, and how it adjusts the rest of its theory of action accordingly (Schön & McDonald, 1998). The reader will infer from the stories we tell in this book, and from the observations of people we interviewed, that such reflection and organizational learning are characteristic of the ATLAS organizations.

However, it was well beyond our capacity and the scope of our inquiry to document the degrees of such tendency in each organization. Our purpose was not evaluative. Instead, we used Schön's concept of theory in use in a much more restrictive way. We applied it to what the organizational staff who work for change in schools say they actually do—the *moves* they report. Of course, we know that what people say they do and what they actually do are often different, and we presume that this is no less true in the case of school reform activists. We even know that what people say they do and what they may allow to be put into print about what they say they do—given the political nature of this work—are also different in some cases. These circumstances have limited the reach of our work, and the reader should bear this in mind. Nevertheless, we believe that we have managed in this book to reach a level of intimacy in reporting on contemporary school reform that is unusual and that the reader will find particularly informative and useful.

In the chapters that follow, the reader will find verbal evidence of both of the analytical structures we used. On the one hand, we like the plainness of *principles, strategies,* and *moves*—and think they help the reader keep better track of the elements of the complex organizations we depict. On the other hand, we need the complexity of the three layers—espoused theory, design theory, and theory in use—of Schön's analytical structure.

ORGANIZATION OF THE BOOK

We report our Seminar findings in four chapters, each focused on one of the four ATLAS organizations. Each chapter is the product of a research and writing collaboration between some outsiders and at least one insider. Thus, for the chapter on Project Zero, Nancy Ames played the outsider, and she conducted the interviews and the staff room seminar. But Tom Hatch and Ed Kirby, the insiders, participated closely in her work. They suggested interviewees who might offer a helpful range of views, helped her interpret her findings, helped with the design of the chapter, arranged for an inside dialogue about the portrayal in order to validate it, and contributed some writing. A similar division of responsibilities characterized the construction of the other chapters. Hatch played the outsider in the School Development Program chapter along with Joe McDonald, while Norris Haynes and Ed Joyner shared the insider's role. Michael Ben-Avie also played a crucial role in completing this chapter. Ed Kirby was outsider for the Coalition chapter, and Joe McDonald insider. McDonald then played outsider opposite Nancy Ames for the EDC chapter. Throughout the period of research, the co-authors met monthly in the ATLAS Seminar, and in the wise company of James Comer as well as other colleagues, we discussed what we were finding and concluding. During the first year of our work, we also benefited from the company and observations of Mary Metz, a member of a Review Team advising the Seminar. Later, Ted Sizer, Howard Gardner, and Janet Whitla joined in our work and, together with Comer, contributed the Afterword.

Besides the four chapters focused on each of the ATLAS partner organizations, however, the book also has a fifth chapter, this one focused on the organization they spawned, ATLAS itself. It not only presents ATLAS as it has become, but also looks closely at its process of becoming. In this sense, it is about what happens when one tries to pool wisdom about school reform. This chapter too is a collaborative effort—of Tom Hatch and Joe McDonald—and it is based partly on the research of the ATLAS Seminar Ethnography Team composed of Donna Muncey, Karen Fanning, and Noel White. Some data from interviews conducted by the ethnographers show up in other chapters as well. Finally, the introduction you are reading is a collaborative effort of Tom Hatch and Joe McDonald. All of the authors received drafts of all the chapters and had an opportunity to contribute to the final editing. McDonald undertook this editing with assistance from Hatch and Kirby.

We think the reader will find this book more coherent overall in both its tone and style than many books with multiple authors. Nevertheless, there are certain differences among the chapters that we would like to point out here—particularly for the sake of the reader who likes to read chapters in other than the intended order. In writing and editing Chapters 2 and 3, we were intrigued with the contrasts between two organizations that on the surface seem so similar, namely, the School Development Program and the Coalition of Essential Schools. To appreciate these contrasts, and to consider how they may reflect larger tendencies of American school reform, we recommend that the reader read these two chapters together, in whatever order. Chapter 4 is about a school reform venture that derived from a research program. The contrasts that matter here are first of all the internal one—between the cultures of activism and of research—and second an implied one—between the way Project Zero seeks to situate its work in practice and the more typical ways of applied research. In Chapter 5, although we tell the organizational story of Education Development Center, we especially focus on the craft of some of the organization's most senior staff. Readers interested in craft knowledge of change will find this chapter particularly revealing. Finally, Chapter 6—an honest account of the struggle of the other four organizations to "become ATLAS," and also a portrait of the fifth organization born of the effort—is a story that we think embeds several important policy lessons for American school reform. Together with what follows in the rest of this chapter, Chapter 6 can be read as a freestanding story—albeit with the nuances much reduced.

THE FOUR ATLAS PARTNERS

In order to put to good use in their own contexts the theories of action portrayed in this book, readers must not only become acquainted with them, but also reflect on their similarities and differences. Depicting these theories of action in their own unique terms is the special burden of Chapters 2 through 5, as we explained above. However, we also take up the burden here—although briefly, in the manner of the overture to the score rather than the score itself—in order to highlight the similarities and differences. We think presenting these similarities and differences upfront will help the reader think more clearly and more critically about Chapters 2 through 5. Moreover, presenting them lightly here will prepare the reader to explore them more thoroughly in Chapter 6.

Obviously, the ATLAS organizations share enough of a common vision about school change to have sought each other out when the New American Schools Development Corporation issued its call for new school designs. A key element of this common vision is a faith in human development, a rejection of what James Comer in the ATLAS Seminar called the "Calvinist fallacy" that children are more or less fixed in their intellect, moral power, and destiny. These organizations believe that all children can be taught to become intellectually powerful and morally responsible adults. From the perspective of the current system of American schooling, with its immense disparities of expectation and support for children from different backgrounds, this is a radical idea. It is especially their radicalism in this regard that brought these organizations together. But other circumstances helped too. All four organizations had experienced a near exponential growth in their school reform activities as a result of the American enthusiasm for school reform in the late 1980s and early 1990s—particularly school reform that might somehow combine equity and excellence. All four organizations had national reputations and a national clientele, and each had a strong and workable set of strategies in place for serving this clientele. In short, all four were successful and confident organizations. At the same time, however, beneath the patina of their great success, they were all similarly uncomfortable with what they perceived to be gaps in their methodologies and gaps in their understanding of change. Moreover, their collaboration in ATLAS grew out of a mutual sense of isolation. In the early days of ATLAS, Comer often talked of the "lonely business" of school reform and of his desire to work with others experienced in the same struggle. It was useful in this regard that at the beginning of their ATLAS association, all four organizations had their bases of operation in New England, less than a 3-hour drive from each other.[3] They could work together without great investments in airplane tickets and hotel rooms. In particular, their leaders could spend enough time together to get to know each other and learn from each other. And one great fruit of the ATLAS partnership is that they did.

School Development Program

James Comer (1980) traces some of the ideas embodied in the School Development Program to his experiences growing up as an African American in the Midwest.

> In 1939, I entered an elementary school in East Chicago, Indiana, with three other black youngsters from a low-income community. The school was considered one of the best in the district, it was racially integrated and served

the highest socioeconomic group in town. All four of us were from two-parent families, and our fathers made a living wage in the local steel mill. We were not burdened by any of the disadvantages—school segregation, inadequate schools, single-parent families, unemployment—commonly cited as causes of educational underachievement in poor black children. Yet in spite of the fact that we had similar intellectual potential, my three friends have had difficult lives: one died prematurely from alcoholism, a second spent a large part of his life in jail, and a third has been in and out of mental institutions.

Why did my life turn out better? I think it was largely because my parents, unlike those of my friends, gave me the social skills and confidence that enabled me to take advantage of educational opportunities. For example, I became friendly with my third grade teacher, with whom I would walk hand in hand to school everyday. My parents took me to the library so that I could read many books. My three friends, however, never read books—which frustrated and angered their teachers. What their teachers did not realize was that their parents were afraid to go to the library; indeed, they were uncomfortable around white people in general and avoided them. (pp. 42–43)

In 1968, as a professor of psychiatry at Yale Medical School, Comer began a collaboration among two New Haven schools and some colleagues at the Yale Child Study Center. This collaboration was the beginning of the School Development Program, and it owed much to Comer's analysis of his own comparatively advantaged Indiana childhood. It is not enough for children to have well-intentioned schools and good families, he reasoned, if the two exist on separate plains of experience. Yet, in these first schools, he found "no mechanism at the building level to allow parents, teachers, and administrators first to understand the needs, then to collaborate with and help each other address them in an integrated, coordinated way." What was clearly missing for him, and what he and his colleagues and school partners set out to supply, was the "synergism that develops when people work together to address problems and opportunities" (Comer, 1994, p. 3). The result of their efforts was the design of an organizational and management system based on knowledge of child development. This would evolve into what SDP calls the Comer Process.

The Process is based on nine design elements (described in greater detail in Chapter 2). The nine include principles, mechanisms, and operations. SDP's shorthand for the principles is the phrase "collaboration, consensus, and no-fault." Underlying the phrase is an explicit theory of the proper role of schooling in children's development. It suggests that all of a community's caregivers must collaborate in the effort to support this development, that they therefore must learn to listen to and appreciate each other's diverse perspectives, and that they must get out of the habit of assigning blame when things go wrong. The three mechanisms in the

Process are the School Planning and Management Team, the Student and Staff Support Team, and the Parent Team. The School Planning and Management Team, composed of representatives of all of the school's adult stakeholders, is the central mechanism and oversees three operations: the development of a comprehensive school plan, the management of a corresponding staff development plan, and regular assessment to inform goal setting and monitor progress in achieving the plan's goals. The Student and Staff Support Team identifies school procedures and practices that are harmful to students, staff, and parents, and it facilitates changes in these. It also seeks to address individual student behavior problems. Finally, the Parent Team plans and supports a variety of activities that are designed to inform parents about the work of the school, bring less involved parents into the work of the school, and improve the school climate.

Since its origins in 1968, the School Development Program has grown from a small staff working in a few schools into a national initiative partnered with a wide range of schools and districts across the United States. While undergoing such growth, SDP has created a diverse staff in background as well as professional expertise. It makes a point of the fact that in ethnic and racial diversity its staff reflects the clientele it aims ultimately to serve—namely, American schoolchildren.

In the early 1980s, SDP began its growth spurt into a large school reform network when it received funding to support the dissemination of the Comer Process through videotapes, written materials, and training sessions. One SDP senior staff member recalled for us that dissemination "had a capital *D*" at SDP in these years. Much energy went into the production and distribution of newsletters, articles, teleconferences, support materials, and training institutes. Soon, however, the organization faced up to the predictable dilemma of implementation: Putting good ideas into practice is much harder than putting them into currency. The shift from dissemination to implementation at SDP led the organization to form alliances with state departments of education and university schools of education in order to create and support local implementation. It also led to the establishment of regional training centers in several parts of the country. The training centers were designed to create clusters of schools that could share the costs of implementation and share the human resources and knowledge needed to make implementation successful.

This decentralized training strategy offered some relief to an overburdened New Haven staff, but it did not fully address the implementation problems. Some of the regional training centers had jurisdictions as large as New Haven once had, and they also proved costly to maintain. Meanwhile, SDP's research on implementation began to detect serious implementation problems within districts. To address these in the early 1990s,

SDP entered still another phase of its own development, one that it termed "systemic." That is, it began to work with whole districts—often large urban ones like Washington, DC, New Orleans, San Diego, and Oakland—and it began to advocate the organizational redesign of central offices as well as schools. At about this time as well, it began to work more explicitly on curricular and instructional improvement efforts. These had always been the focus of individual schools' comprehensive school plans, but beginning in the early 1990s, SDP as an organization put greater emphasis on such features of systemic accountability as academic learning time, curriculum alignment, and the improvement of standardized test scores (Squires & Joyner, 1996).

The Coalition of Essential Schools

The Coalition of Essential Schools has its roots in a study of high schools (1979–1984), in which CES Chairman Ted Sizer and a small group of researchers investigated the evolution and condition of the American high school. They found that for historically predictable reasons, the high school was failing in three interrelated respects. Its curriculum was disjointed and shallow—lots of coverage of poorly connected subjects, in little depth. Second, it lacked the capacity to know its students well, and it treated them as passive rather than active learners. Third, its teachers worked in isolation from each other and at an unproductively frenetic pace (as many as 190 students to meet in a crammed day). In *Horace's Compromise*, one of three books produced by the study and now a classic of contemporary school reform, Sizer (1984) portrays these problems vividly in the fictional experiences of an English teacher named Horace Smith. Another book out of the study, co-authored by Arthur Powell, Eleanor Farrar, and David Cohen (1985), created an enduring image with its title alone, *The Shopping Mall High School*.

Besides the books it produced, and the attendant publicity they generated about the problems of the high school, the Study of High Schools had another outcome too. Sizer clearly wanted to do more than describe the problems he and his colleagues had found; he wanted to do something about them. An historian and author of an important history of the Committee of Ten (Sizer, 1964), the late-nineteenth-century group that designed the twentieth-century high school, Sizer thought the time might be ripe in the mid-1980s to offer a new design. He invited 12 schools to join him in that effort, and thus CES was launched. Eventually, over 1,000 schools would join the first 12. From the beginning, CES was marked by experimentation and conversation, rather than implementation in the ordinary sense. In contrast to SDP, there has never been a CES Process—

no mechanisms or operations, only Nine Common Principles. The principles build on the central idea that a school's mission should be to help students to learn to use their minds well, and that learning should be a personalized, active, and meaningful experience for both teachers and students.

Just as SDP and its Process has roots in James Comer's personal experiences, CES and its reliance on principles rather than program owes much to Sizer's experiences. He was Dean of the Harvard Graduate School of Education during the heyday of federally inspired school reform in the 1970s. Then in an odd career trajectory, he became headmaster of Phillips Academy, an independent secondary school in Andover, Massachusetts. The first role conditioned him to be skeptical about top-down reform, and the second lent him an abiding empathy for the people who work in schools. As one veteran CES staff member commented, "Ted Sizer believes in teachers more than anyone I know, including teachers themselves." For Sizer, school change is fundamentally local work and must be led by local champions. "Educators, so often criticized, are defensive," he wrote in *Horace's Compromise* (1984). "That most self-styled school reformers are not nor have ever been practicing high school teachers or administrators adds insult to injury. Educators may well ask, How would lawyers react if the rest of us handed them prescriptions for legal reform?" (Sizer, 1984, p. 218). His passions on the subject are always close to the surface and have made him a frequent critic of school reform efforts that seem to him to distrust local capacity. "It is easier," he complained, "for central authority to mandate fifty-four thousand minutes per year than to give discretion to local groups" (Sizer, 1984, p. 218). His prescription, first offered in *Horace's Compromise*, has held steady throughout his chairmanship of CES: "Today there is a sizable core of fine teachers and administrators in our schools. They are often demoralized, but they could, if empowered, lead a renaissance of American high schools: their numbers are large enough" (Sizer, 1984, p. 219).

How large is large enough? Initially, Sizer believed that committed leaders in a handful of redesigned high schools could lead all the others to change. He learned quickly, however, that more schools were needed for at least two reasons: to confront the supposition that only certain contexts could support real change, and to compensate for the fact that the boldest schools sometimes lose out to the fierce opposition they generate. But how might CES hold together a *coalition* as its membership grew—one that would ensure that schools were not left utterly to their own devices? In the early days of CES, this was easy to achieve. The schools' leaders simply gathered together occasionally for conversation around a conference table at Brown University in Providence, Rhode Island, where Sizer was chair of the Education Department and where CES maintained a small staff. And the staff traveled to all the schools periodically to offer direct support. As CES grew, however, other mechanisms had to be devised. No conference table was big enough; indeed, within a few years, no conference center within Rhode Island was big enough. Nor within a short time—and despite considerable philanthropic support—could CES afford to grow a staff large enough to provide direct support to all its member schools. Moreover, CES had to face up to the problem that also confronted SDP: Change-minded schools often bump up against constraints created at the district and state level. School change is never entirely the business of the school alone.

To deal with these dilemmas, CES has pursued three strategies—two in its middle years and one more recently. In 1988, CES joined with the Denver-based Education Commission of the States to create the Re:Learning initiative. Re:Learning was designed to encourage states to establish incentives and policies that would enable CES schools to put the principles into practice. Its motto, emphasizing a shift in the ordinary chain of influence, was "schoolhouse to statehouse." By 1993, it had led to the creation of state-run support centers in 11 states and to a geometric growth in CES membership. Meanwhile, in 1990, CES launched the National Re:Learning Faculty. This project recruited teachers from CES member schools and trained them at Brown as peer consultants, and through an allied effort called the Thompson Fellows Program, created a national cadre of principals of member schools. The idea was that these teachers and principals would help other teachers and principals understand the Nine Common Principles and through their consulting work would "spread the conversation." The combination of the two strategies—Re:Learning itself and the National Re:Learning Faculty—also created a new CES identity, one less centered in Providence. Other entities—namely, state departments of education—now "owned" pieces of the network too, and teachers and principals not just Coalition staff were empowered to offer consultation to the network.

Finally, in 1995, CES announced a third key strategy—one that might be viewed as a logical extension of the previous two. Within a year, it had dismantled its large central staff, formed a "congress" of delegates from regional clusters of member schools, and taken steps to achieve eventual independence from Brown University. The pursuit of this decentralized, network-focused strategy coincided with the establishment at Brown of the Annenberg Institute for School Reform, also headed initially by Sizer. The latter has a broader mission than the Coalition and regards the Coalition as one of a number of national and regional reform efforts that it seeks to support. Still, the existence of the two organizations under the same institutional auspices—and, for a time, sharing the same leader—caused confusion for their staffs, their clients in the field, and the public at large. Today, they are completely separate organizations, and Sizer has given up the directorship of the Institute in order to focus all his energies on the remaking of the Coalition of Essential Schools.

Project Zero

In 1967, during Ted Sizer's deanship at the Harvard Graduate School of Education, the philosopher Nelson Goodman founded a research project there to investigate arts education. Frustrated by the lack of available knowledge about artistic development, Goodman quipped, "We're starting at zero, so we are Project Zero." Howard Gardner and David Perkins, young graduate students at the time of its founding, became Project Zero's co-directors after Goodman's retirement in the early 1970s. They created an amicable division in the project's collective work that has endured for more than 20 years: Perkins, a cognitive psychologist, would lead a Cognitive Skills Group, while Gardner, a developmentalist, would lead the Development Group. Since then, Perkins has led investigations of thinking, problem solving, and creativity. He and his colleagues also have explored issues related to school reform. However, it was Gardner and members of the Development Group who entered into the ATLAS partnership.[4]

Under Gardner's leadership, the Development Group at Project Zero (hereafter called simply PZ) has evolved through three general phases. In the 1970s, much of PZ's work focused on the exploration of developmental perspectives with respect to learning in the arts. Jean Piaget and his theory that children develop their abilities in a predictable series of stages influenced PZ's researchers. Yet they were skeptical as to whether children's abilities in the arts developed in quite the coordinated manner Piaget had suggested. In a longitudinal study of a small group of young children, Gardner and colleagues showed, in fact, that a child's level of development in one area, such as storytelling, did not necessarily reflect his or her level of development in another area, such as drawing or musical perception. Gardner was to combine insights from this research with insights he had acquired from both neuropsychological and intercultural studies that he had conducted elsewhere to formulate a theory of multiple intelligences (or MI theory). He expounded the theory in *Frames of Mind* (1983). In a later book (1993), he reflected on the theory's impact.

> Had I simply noted that human beings possess different talents, this claim would have been uncontroversial—and my book would have gone unnoticed. But I made a deliberate decision to write about "multiple intelligences":

"multiple" to stress an unknown number of separate human capacities, ranging from musical intelligence to the intelligence involved in understanding
oneself; "intelligences" to underscore that these capacities were as fundamental as those historically captured within the IQ test. (p. xi)

Indeed, the book achieved quite a lot of notice, particularly among a group
whose interest Gardner had hardly anticipated. He had added a conclu-
sion to *Frames of Mind*—in response to a funder's suggestion—that briefly
explored the possible implications of MI theory to education, but he had
really aimed the book at his fellow psychologists, not at educators. Yet it
was the latter that responded enthusiastically, as Gardner recalls.

Some months after the publication of *Frames*, I was invited to address the
annual meeting of the National Association of Independent Schools. . . . I
expected the typical audience of fifty to seventy-five persons; a customary
talk of fifty minutes followed by a small number of easily anticipated questions. Instead, arriving at the auditorium a few minutes early, I encountered
a new experience: a much larger hall, entirely filled with people, and hum-
ming with excitement. It was almost as if I had walked by mistake into a talk
given by someone who was famous. (Gardner, 1993, pp. xii–xiii)

In the face of this unanticipated enthusiasm for MI theory among professional educators, Gardner made an important career decision, as he further explains.

I could, I suppose, have closed the *Frames* chapter of my life by returning to
the research laboratory and continuing my experimental studies with children and brain-damaged patients. Alternatively, I could have taken a more
frankly entrepreneurial angle, preparing "tests" of the multiple intelligences,
setting up an organization to promote multiple intelligences, joining the lec-
ture circuit that is populated by educators presenting their wares to a public
all too eager for the latest nostrums. (p. xiii)

Instead, he took a third route, one that ushered in a new phase of PZ's
work: "Working with a large number of colleagues at Harvard Project Zero
. . . I have devoted the bulk of my energies since 1983 to an exploration
of the educational implications of the theory of multiple intelligences"
(p. xiv).

Previously, PZ research had paid almost no attention to schools and
school-based learning. One of the first PZ projects to reverse this emphasis was Project Spectrum. Carried out in collaboration with David Feldman
of Tufts University, it conducted research in preschool classrooms in order
to develop assessments capable of gauging young children's abilities in each

of the different intelligences described in *Frames of Mind*. The researchers quickly found, however, that it was impossible to assess these intelligences fairly without taking into account the opportunities the children had to use them. As a result, rather than simply creating a battery of measures that could be administered in a single sitting, Spectrum developed a variety of activities that could be integrated into the preschool curriculum. These were designed to foster development as well as assess it.

Throughout the 1980s, the interest at PZ in matching curriculum with assessment, and in creating learning opportunities supporting a range of different abilities, showed up in a number of projects, notably Arts PRO-PEL. PROPEL was a collaboration with the Educational Testing Service and the Pittsburgh Public Schools that sought to develop projects and portfolios to assess students' abilities in writing, the visual arts, and music. In addition to broadening the intellectual experiences afforded children in school, PROPEL and other PZ projects at the time sought also to deepen them. This interest was one of the factors that led to the Teaching for Understanding Project. This was inaugurated in 1990 and carried out with David Perkins and colleagues in the Cognitive Skills Group and with Vito Perrone, a Harvard professor who was then director of the Harvard teacher preparation programs (Blythe, 1997; Wiske, 1997).

Obviously, PZ came to the ATLAS partnership on a different path than the one that SDP and CES had traveled. PZ was founded as a think tank, not a school reform network. Researchers, not activists, staffed it. Once committed to exploring the practical dimensions of its own theories, however, PZ quickly perceived the complexities of classrooms and schools and the consequent challenge of changing them. Researchers involved in one PZ project designed to help teachers develop and use portfolios ran into considerable opposition from a small group of parents in one school and saw teachers' efforts derailed in other schools when leadership changed. Teachers collaborating with PZ in the development of activities to promote teaching for understanding found themselves constrained by the rigidities of time in school and by curriculum requirements that promoted superficial coverage of a wide range of topics. Those interested in using the Spectrum materials or developing activities related to the multiple intelligences found that they had to confront the norm of isolation in school and had to learn to work together in teaching teams and to call on parents, volunteers, and others for support.

Thus in the 1990s, PZ entered a third phase of work in which several projects focus on developing the strategies and resources necessary to support the successful application of research and research-based materials in schools. In effect, PZ added activism to its research agenda. In the process, its staff has gained activist credentials. Those involved, for example, in PZ's recent effort to build and sustain a network of reform-focused schools in Massachusetts, underwent experiences quite like those of many of their ATLAS colleagues at SDP and CES. Their voices, raised in this book, have a similar ring. Yet PZ remains unique in other respects. It is still primarily a research-based organization, however activist in its leanings. And nearly all its staff remains deeply interested in learning in the arts.

Education Development Center

Today, the institutional home of the ATLAS Program is Education Development Center in Newton, Massachusetts. Here ATLAS has its office beside many other projects in education that together occupy several EDC buildings converted from old New England mills. In contrast to the three other organizations that created ATLAS, EDC is massive and not easily associated with a single person or easily described in a single narrative of development. Moreover, unlike its partners, it has tended to avoid the spotlight and is therefore more difficult to know. This habit is partly a matter of style. It is also partly a matter of shyness acquired in the wake of conservative opposition to its 1960s social studies curriculum, Man: A Course of Study. This opposition reached Congress and nearly brought an end to the National Science Foundation's support of precollegiate curriculum development (Dow, 1991).

Begun in 1958 as Educational Services Incorporated (ESI), EDC has grown steadily from an original focus on curriculum development to work that mirrors the broad range of issues affecting children's development. Its first effort was to design a new high school physics course, an effort led by Jerrold Zacharias, MIT physicist and veteran of the Manhattan Project, which built the first atomic bomb. Peter Dow (1991) suggests that the new organization, founded by Zacharias and other academics from MIT and Harvard, "attacked the curriculum challenge with the confidence of those who had mastered radar and the atom bomb" (p. 28). From physics, they went on to create curriculum in a variety of areas, all the while presuming that curriculum could transform schooling as technical innovations were then transforming so many other aspects of American life.

Within a few years, however, the members of the young organization had managed to acquire a sense of the differences between curriculum and other technologies and also between education and other industries. They recognized the fundamental dependence of curriculum on interactions between teachers and groups of children. Transformation in such a field, they concluded, requires a host of interrelated innovations of structure, culture, and expertise, and these in turn demand deep learning and unlearning among many people playing many roles.

In an implicit acknowledgment of the greater breadth of the problem that concerned it, ESI merged in 1967 with the Institute for Educational Innovation (IEI)—the first federally funded regional education lab in New England. The result was EDC. The new organization combined ESI's curriculum reforms with IEI's efforts to build capacity in schools to carry out such reforms. Thus before any of its other ATLAS partners was even a year old, EDC already had experienced its first strategic shift and had begun a long effort to adjust its change efforts to the actual complexities of their target. Over the following 30 years, EDC has grown into a large nonprofit corporation with over 200 different projects in education and other areas of human development, a correspondingly large staff, and operations throughout the world. Its president for the past 17 years, Janet Whitla, presides over nearly 400 staff members that include curriculum and policy designers, researchers, and practitioners from a great variety of fields. But most EDC staff members, like many of their colleagues at SDP and CES, are also activists, and of a particular stripe. Whitla characterizes them as question posers. Founded by scientists, the organization has continued to maintain a focus on inquiry, although, as Whitla (1996) has written, inquiry is crucial not only to science, but also to storytelling, poetry making, and leadership. In saying so, she suggests the influence of her own leadership over time and suggests also why no one at EDC today compares school reform with mastering radar and the atom bomb.

To understand EDC as a strategic actor in educational reform, it helps to view its efforts overall as streams of work that sometimes intersect but often proceed in parallel. Each stream has its characteristic strategies. So, for example, EDC has continued its earliest work in the area of curriculum reform, combining it since the mid-1970s with efforts to build capacity for using intellectually powerful and discipline-rich curriculum. Often EDC's capacity building involves district- and state-level initiatives, although it is always focused too on schools and the practices of individual teachers. In addition to providing or brokering the provision of professional development programs for teachers, EDC has helped build and sustain important teacher networks like the Ford Foundation-funded Urban Math Collaboratives. And it also has long provided support for federally funded and other large-scale educational programs—for example, providing training and other support for Head Start since that program's inception in the mid-1960s. Such work has a subtle quality that marks it as change-focused, developmentally sophisticated, and unmistakably EDC. Training materials pose such questions as, "What is developmentally appropriate practice for a Head Start Center?" or "What does it mean to contribute to the growth and development of the whole child?" Finally, EDC also has long been active in policy work, particularly policy work behind the scenes to support educational change. It often facilitates efforts to create connections and to pool expertise and resources across agencies, states, and regions in support of specific initiatives. Frequently, observers of the initiatives do not know that EDC is even involved. In such work, EDC helps create common research agendas, develop collegial networks, identify common problems, and share data on how to solve problems.

DIFFERENCES THAT MAKE A DIFFERENCE

Given their different histories, the ATLAS partners came together knowing they had different perspectives. The reader may already have inferred some of the more interesting of these from the brief descriptions of the organizations offered above. In what follows, however, we make them explicit. We do so because we think they represent more than differences among these four organizations, but reflect as well some faultlines that run throughout late-twentieth-century American school reform—whether behind the scenes or out front. Highlighting them here may help our readers notice them elsewhere too—perhaps within their own reform work, or between their own assumptions and those of some associates. Mind you, we are not suggesting that such faultlines can be easily repaired and the different theories of action that cause them easily harmonized—or even that one should attempt to do so. Knowing where they are, is important, but one often has to learn to live with them. Certainly anything as big and complex as a new system of schooling for the American twenty-first century will have to be built across them. Nor are we suggesting that the usefulness of this book as a source of craft knowledge requires that readers adopt a particular perspective first. One can, for example, choose to imitate EDC's Cathy Morocco in helping teachers to think about their practice, or SDP's Valerie Maholmes in building friendly and honest relations with school leaders, without first deciding what political slant to take on school reform or indeed whether to take a political slant at all. And so it is also with nearly all the other "moves" described in the book. Yet why Morocco or Maholmes tend to work as they do, why they choose to start where they start, and how they measure their own progress in helping to make change happen are all more than matters of intuition and personal style—although these are important influences. They also represent different theories of action.

Any number of possible lenses might serve to reveal important differences in the theories of action of the four ATLAS organizations. For example, in sketching their strategic histories above, we relied to some extent on a personal lens—one that brought into focus Comer's roots, Sizer's career trajectory, Gardner's reaction to the success of his MI theory, and Whitla's humane view of science. For our purposes here, however, we think one may gain the best contrasts by viewing these organizations through either a political or a developmental lens—or, as in what follows, through both. We use both to help compensate for the unavoidable distortion of either.

Political Differences

Given its origins in aesthetics and developmental psychology, it is not surprising that PZ is the least likely of the four ATLAS organizations to construct its work in explicitly political terms. The ideas that drive PZ's work are the product of investigations of human difference but at a personal rather than a group level. These investigations have tended to focus on the developmental trajectories of particular children. Moreover, as PZ has grown in its interest in the educational contexts of development, it has nonetheless tended to see and to act on these contexts with the perspective of the individual child still in mind: What kinds of teaching does the child need? What kinds of assessment? Because PZ's identity is as a research organization, it implicitly thinks that the answers it can construct for such questions can to some extent hover above the messiness of actually acting on the answers. It is in acting that one finds oneself forced to create political as well as developmental strategy, and PZ for the most part leaves that to others, especially those who may be persuaded by its findings and inspired thereby to act on their own contexts. Even where PZ has agreed to take on a whole-school change agenda, and to function as reform coach for some set of schools—as in its recent work with some Massachusetts schools—it typically has constrained the set of schools as one would a research sample. This is in contrast to wanting to expand it as much as possible to heighten the political impact. Its ATLAS partners have a different history in this regard.

Although development is EDC's middle name, the organization also has deep political roots. EDC was founded on a perception that curriculum in the United States was too parochial. Its founders fashioned an implicitly political response: to persuade local authorities to be guided by national expertise. They sought to bring to the schools the influence of the best current thinking in the disciplines and the most up-to-date theories of child development. This is part of what Peter Dow (1991) means in saying that they brought to the problems of schooling the same inclination that others in that era brought to aviation or defense development. This is what has been called the "skunks work" option—to get the best "brains" to pool their brain power and to focus it on a single problem, such as what to teach in science. EDC's earliest curriculum designers included some of the nation's most accomplished scholars and psychologists. Although it later abandoned its strategy of relying on academic stars as well as on the mere diffusion of best thinking, EDC has never lost its sense that at least part of the problem that reformers of American education face is entrenched localism. "How do you create a common civic culture in a country this diverse?" asks Janet Whitla. "How do you keep people talking with one another across all these variations in geography, race, and culture?" Moreover, how do you ensure that common knowledge bases in education emerge and are used, and "that people don't have to re-invent the wheel over and over again?" As a result of the fact that much of EDC's work over the years has focused on disadvantaged children and communities, both in the United States and in the developing world, Whitla is concerned too about the tendency of localism to mask and sustain inequalities.

Ted Sizer's political instincts draw him also toward disadvantaged communities, but he and CES distrust the capacity of nonlocal authorities to make things better for such communities. In fact, he attributes a good amount of the disadvantage that many American children suffer in schools —particularly in big cities—to the overgrown systems that govern them. He has been deeply influenced in this regard by his closest colleague in reform, Deborah Meier. She helped launch the small schools movement in New York City and has been a champion in both New York and Boston of charter districts or autonomous networks of small schools within otherwise large bureaucratic school systems. Sizer, an historian, seems radical in his prescriptions for the reform of the American system of schooling only when one fails to take the long view. From an historical perspective, he is the conservative who wishes to stop the movement of that system toward greater and greater central authority. He thinks the consequences of this movement are alienation on the part of local communities and parents, and apathy on the part of schools with respect to their duty toward particular children. "Inspiration, hunger: these are the qualities that drive good schools," he says. "The best we educational planners can do is to create the most likely conditions for them to flourish, and then get out of their way." It is of the greatest political importance to him that parents retain, as he has said repeatedly, the right to speak directly to, and if necessary argue with, whoever has the power to decide what their children must learn. Sizer's own teaching and his scholarship have concerned the high school, which for many reasons—including consolidation drives, college and career expectations, and the distance that adolescents like to gain on their families—are especially susceptible to the kind of alienation he seeks to dispel.

Much of the educational innovation of the twentieth century has fa-vored consolidation of local schools, the assumption of greater district and then greater state responsibility and authority, and the kind of national-ization of curricular perspectives that EDC has championed. In such a context, Sizer's prescriptions for smallness and the enhancement of pa-rental authority can seem radical rather than conservative. Moreover, to Jim Comer's ears at least, they can seem somewhat menacing. In response to a remark that the past 10 years have been an exciting time of experi-mentation for American schools, Comer quipped: "That's chaos you're looking at out there, not experimentation." He agrees with Sizer that communities need to have ownership of their own schools and of the educational initiatives that occur there, but he thinks this can be achieved through the inclusion of voices rather than the devolution of authority. From his perspective, the right political questions are how to make the system work for everyone and how to give all stakeholders a voice in its decision making. It is a matter of sharing power, not shifting it. So many American communities are already so fragile, he says, that dismantling the educational system involves too big a risk. His view is historical too: Quite apart from whatever impact it has had on the quality of American teaching and learning overall, the twentieth-century growth of central authority in education has tended to favor the fight for equity. It was fed-eral authority that outlawed deliberate racial segregation and gender dis-crimination, that introduced Headstart and school lunch programs, that provided equity in welfare and health care benefits for the poor, and that took the first efforts through Title One to direct funds toward the most educationally disadvantaged students. And it is at the state level where the legal and political challenges to funding inequities among schools are being waged. Sizer likes to explain the difference in political perspective between himself and his friend as predominantly a function of where their reform experience has been especially concentrated. Comer has worked mostly with elementary schools, he says. However, from the perspective of high schools—particularly urban high schools—it is hard, Sizer argues, to prefer the status quo even to the most "chaotic" experiments.

Developmental Differences

Taking up the developmental lens, one sees a different pattern. Here PZ cedes its place as least interested to CES, which tends to be as "a-develop-mental" as PZ is apolitical. Not surprisingly, one reason is political. CES is wary about who gets targeted for development work. It knows that in the ordinary parlance of American schooling, the word *development* teamed with the word *professional* frequently denotes a process that disempowers teachers—as in, "We had our teachers inserviced." Similarly, CES fears that efforts to define in systematic ways the route of a school's development, might usurp the school's power to define a unique route. "No two good schools are alike," Ted Sizer likes to say, and the practice at CES has been to assume as well that no two schools grow toward goodness in quite the same way. By contrast, SDP is far more doctrinal. It has the Comer Process and an elaborate implementation design. CES not only expects schools to put the Nine Common Principles into practice in their own way, but it even has been reluctant to suggest options for doing this. It has tended to rely instead on the exchange of school visits among member schools, on consulting by the leaders of experienced schools, on rich stories of practice published in its periodical *Horace*, and on a massive yearly gathering called the Fall Forum. Here the workshops are nearly all run by teachers and principals who, in Ted Sizer's characterization, "give witness." Meanwhile, it is important to note that the target of interest is always the school: CES is a coalition of member schools, not member educators. The difference is important for many reasons, not the least of which is that it tends to define the process of development in organizational rather than psychological terms.

The other ATLAS partners view school reform differently. PZ and EDC, for example, tend to see it from the child and the teacher up. The question is nearly instinctual with them: How do people develop the skills and understandings they need to be effective teachers and learners? This is fundamentally a psychological question—one that suggests the influences on PZ and EDC of psychologists like Jean Piaget and Jerome Bruner. It has led to the deep interest at PZ and EDC in the meaning and process of understanding, in the design of a pedagogy of understanding, and in the development of contexts to foster understanding. This is, of course, a trajectory of interest that leads toward matters organizational, but where it starts makes all the difference.

At SDP, *development* has a somewhat different, although no less central, meaning. This is the meaning that arises from child psychiatry, public health, and the historical African American experience. At SDP, the developmental psychology that undergirds the EDC and PZ perspectives is replaced by a clinical psychology that puts more emphasis on social, emotional, and moral factors in healthy development, and that highlights the roles of family and community in supporting such development. As James Comer (1988) explains:

> Many kinds of development, in social, psychological, emotional, moral, linguistic and cognitive areas are critical to future academic learning. The attitudes and behaviors of the family and its social network strongly affect such

development. A child whose development meshes with the mainstream values encountered at school will be prepared to achieve at the level of his or her ability. . . . A child from a poor, marginal family, in contrast is likely to enter school without adequate preparation. (pp. 4–5)

This developmental need creates in turn what SDP regards as a moral obligation. The larger community, including district administrators, as well as parents and community members of all racial and ethnic groups, has a moral obligation to provide the resources, guidance, and direction that individual children need in order to develop fully. SDP's organizational strategies may be seen as efforts to assist people in discharging this obligation.

Differences in Practice

The differences in theory of action among the four organizations are often not noticeable at all when one considers their work from the perspective of a school that has enjoyed a long-standing relationship with one of them. At this level of theory in use, the differences may largely disappear—be absorbed, so to speak, into the school's own, and only partly derivative, theory of action. Nor do we think the differences are so noticeable from the perspective of the vast challenge facing American public education at the turn of the twentieth century. That is because the common beliefs among these four organizations are so much more salient from that perspective—in particular, their focus on the intellectual and moral capacities of all children, and their insistence that adults keep the children in mind. It is also because they share a common history as independent nonprofits whose school reform efforts have spanned years marked by peaks and valleys of governmental interest and funding. This history is partly what lends all four organizations what Civil Rights activist Myles Horton (Horton, Kohl, & Kohl, 1990) would have called their sense of the long haul.

Still, the differences can make a difference in answering such strategic questions as where change efforts should begin, who should be involved, and how much time, attention, and resources should be devoted to different kinds of activities. They also can make a difference in deciding what especially needs changing and how much. For this reason, they did make a difference in the four organizations' efforts to create still a fifth organization—namely, ATLAS itself—and in the efforts of that organization to work with districts and schools. Therefore, we will revisit the question of what difference difference makes in our concluding chapter, entitled "Becoming ATLAS."

CHAPTER 2

Inside the School Development Program

For more than a quarter of a century, the School Development Program at Yale University, founded and led by James P. Comer, M.D., has worked behind the scenes of American school reform to promote learning through healthy child development. To help schools foster healthy child development, SDP prescribes a supportive fabric of relationships; then, by various means that are both patient and insistent, it helps schools create such a fabric. In this chapter, we will explore what exactly SDP prescribes and why, and also how it goes about helping.

We begin with several assumptions crucial to SDP's espoused theory of action. A first set concerns the nature of the problem of American schooling, as SDP sees it, and of its preferred solution. When talking to parents and educators about schooling and its problems, James Comer uses different metaphors to evoke different parts of a system working in collaboration. He sometimes uses a physical image: "We have a thousand engines all churning independently, but how do you put everything together to help children grow?" And sometimes he uses an epidemiological image: "My public health training taught me that lots of things must come together to cause disease and to prevent disease." One assumption revealed in these images is that the American educational system is dysfunctional now for many American children because it is not well coordinated to serve their healthy growth. A second is conveyed in the choice of metaphors: The engines can be synchronized, the disease turned back, because the problem of school change is a rational problem. Many educators say there is no science of education, Comer told us, but they are wrong. "Child development should be the basic science of education in the way that anatomy and physiology and chemistry are the basic sciences of medicine. When you put the basic sciences together in medicine it allows you to think and apply your knowledge to clinical situations." Similarly, he added, "child development can help us think about curriculum, instruction, teacher preparation, assessment, and everything else."

A second set of assumptions in SDP's espoused theory of action grew out of Comer's own therapeutic training and skills, according to Donald Cohen, the current Director of the Yale Child Study Center, and Cohen's predecessor, Albert Solnit. In particular, they mention Comer's "clinical talent for quiet observation, attentive listening, and respectful collaboration" (Comer, Haynes, Joyner, & Ben-Avie, 1996, p. xii). One assumption is that neither schools as organizations nor the people who work in them can be forced to change, even by means of the most cleverly devised sanctions and incentives. Another is that meaningful change requires structures to facilitate personal and organizational growth. A third is that it also requires patience. These assumptions play out not only in SDP's espoused theory—with its rhetorical emphasis on "collaboration, consensus, and no-fault"—but in the design of the Comer Process and in the theory in use some SDP staff members described for us. It plays out too in the organization's larger efforts—especially through Comer's writing and speaking—to influence the direction of American school reform generally. As Ed Joyner likes to put it, Comer "whispers in the ear of America that we can be a better nation than we are now, that we can do a better job for children." Although his message is no less insistent for the whisper, he "doesn't yell and scream," Joyner told us. He speaks even critical words in a quiet, reflective voice—a therapist's voice.

PARADOXES OF REFORM

At times SDP can seem paradoxical. For example, there is the strong scientific attitude in the organization, expressed in its medical and psychiatric allusions, its long-established research program, and its view of itself as data-driven. On the other hand, there is also SDP the movement, the sense that the organization projects of an effort big enough to help the most dispirited school community to empower itself on behalf of its children. Second, there is the realism in SDP's stance toward schools that makes it the most accepting, among the ATLAS partners, of schools as they are. On the other hand, there is a passion for change that evokes the Civil Rights movement. "It's a paradoxical challenge," as Director of Professional Development and Consultation Jack Gillette put it, "to be totally supportive of where people are," on the one hand, and to have as well an "absolutely unrelenting passion to move forward." Yet the impulses are not inherently contradictory and indeed co-exist in most religions, psychotherapies, and healthy helping relationships of all kinds. Still, "it's enormously difficult to stay in the middle," Gillette claimed. "You become coopted if you're too far on the accepting side, if you understand all the reasons why people are bitter about kids or bitter about the bureaucracy or whatever. But if you're too much on the other side, you're just a soapbox."

The principled effort to "stay in the middle," as Gillette put it, characterizes most of SDP's strategies as school reformer. In what follows, we examine the organization at the strategic level by means of a close look at five strategies that seem to us central to its work. The first three build on what SDP calls the Comer Process: training in the process, coaching those trained in the process, and building wider relationships that mirror the process. The fourth concerns the movement side of SDP, and the fifth involves SDP's approach to systemic reform. In all of these strategies, one can detect the tugs of apparently contrary impulses: to be critical and supportive, to be realistic and hopeful, to insist and to whisper.

TRAINING IN THE COMER PROCESS

The Comer Process seems aptly named given its roots in James Comer's work and also in his life experience. His mother, Maggie Comer, created a family context that motivated and prepared Comer and his siblings to function and succeed in mainstream society. "My mother used to say," he told us, "that if you act like that window on the third floor is a door, you're going to have a problem." The lesson concerned the benefits of behaving in socially acceptable ways. As Comer often observes, his parents made it possible for him to gain access to the educational and economic benefits of mainstream society, although they themselves were poorly educated working-class people. In turn, his own life experience of feeling connected to the social mainstream from earliest childhood, and of using the connection to achieve adult success, has framed both Comer's educational philosophy and his sense of schooling's shortcomings.

A major premise of the Comer Process is that schools too can help build children's connections to the social mainstream. This is because schools are by definition helping institutions, because in urban communities they are often one of the few bridges between economically marginal families and the mainstream, and because—at least in theory—they are themselves communities where professionals and parents and other caregivers can intersect. Yet, as Comer discovered when he began to work with the New Haven schools in the late 1960s, schools are rarely in the habit of helping students build the connections they need for healthy development. One reason for the rarity, he concluded then, was the lack of any means at the building level to bring parents, teachers, and administrators together regularly in ways that would enable them to understand each other's perspectives and to work together in the interests of children's development. What he and his colleagues and school partners set out to do—first in New Haven—was to supply such means. The result was the Comer Process.

It has a complex design involving nine elements: three teams, three principles, and three operations.

Teams

- *School Planning and Management Team (SPMT)*. This is composed of representative teachers, parents, school support staff, and the principal. The SPMT is the central organizing body of the school and the functional as well as symbolic heart of the Comer Process. It specifies and monitors goals for improving the school's climate and enhancing the academic performance of its students.
- *Student and Staff Support Team (SSST)*. This is composed of school staff with child development and mental health knowledge: guidance counselors, school psychologist, attendance officer, social worker, speech and language therapist, special education teacher, and school nurse. It works closely with the SPMT to address schoolwide psychosocial issues. The goal is to manage student psychosocial issues proactively.
- *Parent Team*. This is composed of parents who are members of the parent association or organization in the school, including those chosen by other parents to represent them on the SPMT. Parent volunteers and those who may be paid stipends for working in the school also are considered to be members of the Parent Team. One purpose of the team as a whole is to ensure that this third group is large and especially includes parents who previously had not been involved because of some discomfort with the school environment. The Team's central purpose is to bridge the gap between school and home.

Principles

- *Collaboration*. This first principle calls for a spirit of cooperation in school decision making that honors diverse points of view.
- *Consensus*. The second insists that diverse voices be heard and the interests they represent accommodated. It discourages voting on the grounds that it can weaken the losers' stake in carrying out the decisions reached.
- *No-fault*. The third principle insists that the school eschew the ordinary school habit of assigning blame in the process of analyzing and solving problems.

Operations

- *Comprehensive school plan.* Developed by the School Planning and Management Team, this first operation lays out goals for the school's social climate and for the academic achievement of its students.
- *Staff development.* This second operation is planned by the SPMT with help from the district office. The intention is to tie all staff development to the School Plan and in the process guard against fragmentation and low levels of motivation.
- *Assessment and modification.* A function again of the SPMT, the point of this third operation is to introduce a culture of inquiry into the school—particularly with regard to the actual effects of the School Plan. An important function too is to introduce reflective conversation about the data the inquiry generates.

Underlying all this design is an explicit theory. It derives especially from social psychological and human ecological perspectives (Comer, Haynes, Joyner, & Ben-Avie, 1996), and it is the product of Comer's theoretical efforts over many years, as well as those of other scholars at the Yale Child Study Center. This theory rests especially on the idea that behavior and development are not separate and individual phenomena but consequences of the interaction of an individual and a feeling-laden environment. To change behavior and foster development, therefore, one must understand and act on the context in which they occur. To do this takes concerted effort on the part of all the important players in that context (Comer, Haynes, Joyner, & Ben-Avie, 1996). The Comer Process is principally about making such a concerted effort within school and across the ordinary division between school and home.

One source of the power of the Comer Process, according to SDP staff, is that it rationalizes and operationalizes two things desperately missing in the cellular and frantic world of many schools: collective responsibility and reflection that serves action. The Comer Process obligates the school community to reflect regularly and communally on what it is doing for children, why, and to what effect. And it insists that this reflection lead to action, as well as to successive cycles of reflection and action. Norris Haynes, SDP Director of Research and Evaluation, told us, "We operate on the premise that changing schools requires taking a critical look at what's being done and what could be done better." To this end, the research division of SDP has developed a wide range of tools and techniques, including surveys of school climate, to help schools and districts develop appropriate plans for action.

Training in the Comer Process is considered to be the first step in what Ed Joyner described for us as a three-step induction into SDP. "We train a person and then we have a relationship with that person that is a coaching relationship. Finally, after a period of time, we develop a peer relationship."

SDP's professional development training programs include a Principal's Academy that is designed for the principals of schools in the early stages of implementation, and week-long training institutes held primarily at Yale but also in school districts. The week-long training institutes, known popularly within SDP as 101 and 102, are designed for SDP facilitators, parents, school staff, community members, and others who have a stake in the success of the students.

SDP also has formed training partnerships with institutions like Southern University at New Orleans, San Francisco State University, and Cleveland State University. These partnerships link the schools of education, local school districts, organizations such as alumni associations, and SDP. In *Rallying the Whole Village*, Debra Smith and Louise Kaltenbaugh (1996) describe how these partnerships link the pre-professional teacher education programs at regionally important teacher training institutions with the continuing professional development needs of local SDP schools.

What happens in a formal SDP training session? Participants are assembled into adult learning groups. The emphasis is on process and content: The Comer Process is modeled by the trainers, and the content focuses on child and adult development as well as methods of implementation. SDP Implementation Coordinator Pat Howley told us that he likes to engage in simulations.

> I like to say things like, "Let's have a School Planning and Management Team meeting right here." Once we had teams being trained from four schools, and I said, "I'd like you to pick a representative from each of your teams to meet with me and you can observe the meeting that we have." In the meeting, we asked how the training was going and what would they change about the training. "Find out what the other people say," I told them, "and come back and we'll have another meeting." In that small way I simulated the experience of representing a group of other people. By the end of the week, most of the people at that training were ready to be a School Planning and Management Team.

Other training experiences include discussions of case studies drawn from SDP-affiliated schools. Here too simulation may be involved, as participants play the role of SPMT members. SDP also has developed specific training modules focused on such topics as how to provide constructive feedback in a nonjudgmental way, how to form leadership teams, and how to manage task forces.

COACHING

First comes training in the Comer Process, then coaching. SDP facilitators serve as coaches who help to answer questions on site, identify problems or concerns as they emerge, and provide guidance and feedback in dealing with them. Originally, staff members at SDP's national office coached each SDP school directly, but today they train facilitators at national professional development academies to do the coaching. These trainees, in turn, train and coach school communities in the implementation of the Comer Process—with the support and consultation of the national office. In signing a memorandum of agreement with SDP, districts agree to hire such facilitators. Typically, the facilitators are people who also play other roles in the district, involving, for example, parent relations, staff development, or community outreach. Jack Gillette told us that when SDP first began to work at a distance from New Haven, it used conventional and more or less didactic training schemes to train local SDP facilitators. The result in many cases, he said, was that it ended up with didactic local agents, and the district ended up with more didactic leadership overall. Such trainees were not only unpersuasive, but they also modeled exactly the wrong message inasmuch as they themselves overlooked the necessity of building relationships first (Gillette & Kranyik, 1996). Now, SDP is more apt to emphasize the "coaching of coaches" rather than the "training" of them.

Pat Howley explained to us what it takes to be a good SDP coach. "I think you have to be comfortable with yourself, and know the process of change and growth in a school and how it takes place." Furthermore, he added, you have to have confidence that the school *will* change, "that it is going to work—especially when there is a lot of pressure." The calculation of pressure must be factored in continuously: "If I go slower, and I try to facilitate their growth, it's going to take 3 weeks," but the particular situation may not be able to afford 3 weeks. The shortcut, he told us, is to say, "Here is what other schools are doing." Yet, Howley feels conflicted about this option whenever he exercises it. With the shortcut, "They feel great—They've got a piece of paper or something to hold onto. But the people who did it the first time did not have this piece of paper and they probably learned more by doing it themselves. But the other side of it says to me, Why re-invent the wheel?" His rule of thumb in such cases is to base the move on an assessment of the group's experience of change. The farther along they are in the change process, he told us, the more likely they will be to think critically about some other school's formulation rather than simply adopt it.

Howley, who is a trained counselor, spoke with us also about a related challenge of coaching: figuring out how much direction and support to provide, while avoiding the establishment of a dependent relationship. "When I work with people and they say, 'Tell me what I am supposed to do here,' I don't bite. I say, 'Tell me what you want to do here. It's your time. What are some of the issues that you are struggling with?' Then they move towards independence. And then we become interdependent as I start learning from them. And I share what I'm seeing going on, and they share what they see going on." Again, a complex calculus of judgment is involved. What are the steps that people need to go through? How much time do they have to go through them? How much pressure is on them? Nor are these questions answerable except with reference to the context. Howley explained, for example, that implementation teams early on are often dependent on the school's principal. Later, however, they are more likely to respond to a principal's suggestion with a line like, Let's look at the pros and cons of that. "When they are at that level," he told us, "I'm more comfortable in saying what I think could happen."

RELATIONSHIP BUILDING

To understand relationship building as an SDP strategy, one has to know that the Comer Process is intended to model good relationships, that it represents a kind of scaffold for building them. "The whole point" of having a Process, Comer once told Jack Gillette, is to help people understand that "in every interaction, you are either building community or breaking community." In this sense, he added, the mechanics of the Process are secondary; they are tools for achieving a trusting environment, an opportunity for all stakeholder voices to be heard and considered with respect, open conversation, and productive feedback.

Comer told us that he did not fully understand the importance of relationship building as a change strategy until SDP worked for the first time with a district that was some distance from New Haven. "We brought in somebody from the district and gave her a year working with us here at Yale," he recalled, but it was a "huge mistake. We hadn't quite grasped the relationship issue." SDP is not something, he explained, that one can "take and put in the heads of people who then put it in the heads of other people." When the person trained at Yale "went back to her district and told them about the model and tried to get them to do it, it didn't work. They said, 'You had that wonderful year at Yale—*you* do it.'" But SDP did not give up in this case. It brought a team of people from this same district for a 3-day training session, and that helped, according to Comer. Then, the next time SDP worked with a district far from New Haven, it invited the district to send somebody to Yale for 1 month only. That's about the right length of time for training, Comer told us, because the trainee can both have a substantial new experience and also keep her relationships intact back in her district.

All the ATLAS partners practice building and sustaining relationships as a principled strategy of school reform, but the others are not so deliberate in their practice as SDP. The deliberateness at SDP is the product of several factors. One is, of course, James Comer's experience as a therapist. SDP's interventions, he has written, ask "for a new way of working and a new way of thinking, and people don't change easily, especially when they are being helped to change by strangers" (Comer, Haynes, Joyner, & Ben-Avie, 1996, p. 5). By this logic, one cannot hope to have any effect whatsoever in one's change efforts until one has built a trusting relationship with the people who must own and enact the change. But on the basis of such a trusting relationship, according to SDP curriculum expert David Squires, one can progress surprisingly far. He told us, for example, the story of one school where the ordinarily tortuous business of aligning curriculum and assessment was accomplished in the space of a year by trading on relationships formed as a result of collaborative planning.

A second factor in SDP's deliberateness in building relationships is its concern with the fragmented quality of many help initiatives in urban school systems. Comer recalls observing an effort that involved nine different people trying to help one child—but differently, separately, without talking to one another, and presumably with different grants funding their work. They "jumped in and out of the classroom, each doing his or her little thing, with the kid pieced up all over the place" (Comer, Haynes, Joyner, & Ben-Avie, 1996, pp. 3–4; see also Schorr, 1988). One can read in such a remark a justification of the mechanisms in the Comer Process— especially the Student and Staff Support Team—where relationships are primarily pragmatic rather than therapeutic, and where they are a prerequisite for getting any work done.

A third factor in SDP's pursuit of relationships is theoretical in the most obvious way. It is the idea that the healthy psychosocial development of each child requires the collaboration of all the adults in that child's life. The whole village cannot rally if it is not in fact a village—that is, if there are no relationships among its members, if segments of it regard other segments as alien and hostile. Although we call this insight theoretical, it has an intuitive facet as well, as Comer pointed out to us—one related to the diversity of the SDP staff. Relationships, he claimed, are "unintentionally underplayed by people who are—deep in their hearts, deep in their upbringings—much more a part of the mainstream. They were never marginal, so they don't understand marginality and exclusion and the power of that." For African Americans, however, and other groups that have been marginalized in American society, a sense of the importance of relationships is "central. It's not abstract. It's not theoretical. It's at the core of our being, and we sense that all kids, all players, have to feel belonging in order to perform at their best."

Moreover, relationships can help form a bridge between the margins and the mainstream. Comer speaks of how his mother managed this feat, and taught him much in the process.

> She worked [as a domestic] for the people in the highest socio-economic group in town, and, in an interesting way, was part of their network. When she wanted jobs, she would get on that telephone and contact the people she worked for. She insisted that people respect her. She was good, and therefore people wanted her and respected her. So when she called it was very important for them to find jobs or do whatever it was she wanted. So I learned a lot about how you work the mainstream and the importance of networking and making contacts and building those networks in life. It was her ability to cross over into the mainstream that allowed me to understand how that system worked.

At the most basic level, Jack Gillette told us that relationship building "means being an ear, listening more than talking." It also means doing the seemingly "little things" that often appear to be extraneous or outside the staff members' implementation responsibilities. Fundamentally, it involves knowing the school. "It seems almost like wasted time," Gillette told us. "You're constantly going to schools. And it's hard not to make them ritual events, but the visits are so important." Where the discipline comes in, he added, is "that schools all look the same at first blush. And you have to really force yourself to see what the uniqueness is and then communicate that back to the people that you're working with. That's part of what really enhances the relationship: that you can come into my school and not just make generic nice comments."

Valerie Maholmes told us that she spends a lot of her time in schools "handholding, and encouraging people." Maholmes even goes to people's homes for dinner. "As the saying goes," she explained, "No one cares what you know until they know that you care." But when they know that, then one can get down to business. "What's paramount," she added, "is putting your cards on the table." If, for example, "your goal is to ensure that the infrastructure is such that it will allow the district-wide implementation of SDP, then you have to say that right off the top. You can't go in saying, 'We want you to do it any way you want,' knowing full well that what you're looking for is a district-wide planning team or a number of other things that are a part of systemic reform for us."

At SDP, networking is an intentional consequence of relationship building, and it becomes in turn a key element of a systemic strategy. Staff members told us that they write letters of recommendation, supply references, and make phone calls in order to help SDP people gain greater positions of authority in their districts. They also work to ensure that those who make hiring decisions in these districts understand SDP and its value, and understand the possible impact of leadership changes on its successful implementation. The consequences of working the network in this way can be dramatic. Pat Howley told us of one network principal who became superintendent in his district: "First, he helped with the transition of a new principal into his old position. And he was also able to name another person to the central office staff, and empowered that person to bring 40 new principals into our program in one year."

Jack Gillette asked us, however, to appreciate that more is involved here than the SDP rolodex. "The core competence you need to be effective in SDP," he claimed, "is also incredibly important for the kind of leadership development that will bring a person from principal to central office to the superintendency." In this sense, SDP training and coaching help individuals recognize the skills they need to be successful and to earn promotions. In the process, the naming and valuing of these skills raises awareness of them in the community as a whole and contributes to a district's overall growth in leadership competence and stability.

SCALING UP

In the first SDP efforts in the New Haven schools, Comer and his colleagues were able to work directly and closely with school and community members. In these early efforts, the key, according to Comer, "was talking with the principals after every School Planning and Management meeting, and helping them understand what was going on, and giving up the control approach and developing the collaborative approach." This was hard for the principals to do, he told us, because it clashed with what they had been conditioned to think of as strong leadership. The SDP team worked "to help them see that they were actually stronger and more effective when they could give up some control and help other people participate. As they saw that and began to do it more and more, we would pull back and say less."

When SDP expanded to sites far from New Haven, however, its staff had to figure out how to work at a distance—without knowing the school and its community intimately, without personally coaching the principal. This is the scaling up problem that has been faced in turn by each of the ATLAS organizations, including most recently ATLAS itself. For SDP, as for the others, it was and continues to be a spur to strategic invention. In dealing with it, SDP sometimes seems like EDC: training and networking local coaches, producing materials to support implementation, and seeking to establish supportive systemic structures at the state and district levels. In one respect, however, it seems more like CES: It has become a member-based organization.[1]

SDP approaches membership gingerly, taking each potential member school and district through pre-membership stages of exploration. Here it seeks to stimulate enough commitment to ensure thoughtful early implementation efforts and at the same time sufficient patience to ride out the inevitable implementation bumps. In other words, it hopes to achieve upfront buy-in. It hopes to avoid as well the kind of thoughtless "adoption" experiences that Joanne Corbin, Director of Operations, described for us, "where SDP was one of several choices schools had for reform, and they chose SDP just because they needed a reform model or they needed to improve their scores." Such schools typically do not understand the Comer Process, she continued. "They may even have chosen it because they flipped a coin."

Interestingly, SDP's strategic commitment to achieving upfront staff commitment and participation has been reinforced, according to Corbin, by experiences with several schools that at first were told that they could not join SDP—in some cases because they had been selected to be in the control group for an external evaluation (Comer, Haynes, Joyner, & Ben-Avie, 1996). The "control" schools began implementing the Comer Process on their own, sending a strong message of commitment. In other cases, schools and districts were asked to delay their formal participation in SDP so as to avoid stretching training and coaching resources too thin. Here, too, some went ahead with implementation on their own. Appreciating the spirit, SDP relented from its original decision to delay membership. The consequences in some cases, according to Corbin, have been high levels of implementation in these schools.

But aside from saying "not yet," how does one generate upfront commitment? The classic way is with a sales pitch. Indeed, Corbin acknowledged that there is some salesmanship in the repertoire of most of her SDP colleagues—as in the repertoire of staff members across the ATLAS partnership. She also told us, however, that she thinks that a sales pitch has only limited use. She has learned not to push too hard, she said, not to go beyond the effort to say simply, "This is the model, this is what we do." If the model is "oversold," she added, misunderstandings often develop about what it really is and how it works.

One alternative to salesmanship is persuading people to become part of something bigger than themselves—to believe in the mission, to join up. It is a classic American change strategy. "If this work is to endure," Ed Joyner told us, "then you have to have a legion of people from all races, creeds, religions, backgrounds, who believe in it." Moreover, the belief has to move beyond school and into the community. Ultimately, Joyner told us, SDP depends on "people who will let that belief be manifested in their work whatever it is, even if it's not in schools."

In explaining the beliefs that sustain SDP the movement, Joyner referred first of all to a belief in the Comer Process—especially in the generalized power of collaboration, consensus decision making, and no-fault problem solving. But he referred also to a belief that infuses the Process, and that James Comer spoke of when he complained to us that "many people don't believe in development. They don't think that children can grow intellectually and morally." Comer believes instead, and SDP accepts as a basic principle, that all children develop continuously along six different developmental pathways. He identifies these as physical, psychological, social, cognitive, ethical, and language. The key to healthy development, he believes, is to attend in a balanced way to these diverse pathways, and to do so collaboratively—that is, by bringing the energies of all significant caregivers to bear. Schools will facilitate this, however, only if they believe that it is worth doing, that the children will indeed develop as a result, that they *can* develop. Too many schools in his judgment think that children are "predestined." These schools are gripped, he told us, by "a Calvinist fallacy."

How to undo this grip? It is generally pointless to confront a fallacy of belief solely with rational argument; one needs a more directly countervailing move. Jack Gillette told us about a local SDP facilitator who is skillful at creating a "ritual acknowledgment" of being in the presence of something bigger than oneself, a collective sense of being moved. "She had almost a thousand people at a Saturday retreat. People were in tears at the end of the day."

But the membership process at SDP is more than a manifestation of the organization's movement side. It is also one place where movement and model intersect. That is because, as we suggested above, there is a specified procedure for joining up, and the procedure reflects the Comer

Process. It begins with discussions involving the superintendent and proceeds to the formation of a district-wide steering committee to investigate further involvement with SDP. Predictably, this central steering committee mirrors the makeup and procedures of the School Planning and Management Team. It deliberately includes union leadership, board members, parents, teachers, principals, and others in the process—gives them all both a voice and an opportunity to examine their unique perspectives on the district's needs. If, after examining the program from its diverse members' own perspectives, the steering committee chooses to implement the program, they are asked to agree to a number of prerequisites established by SDP. The district then signs a contract or "memorandum of understanding" with SDP that outlines these prerequisites. They include shifting key functions from the central office to school sites as School Planning and Management Teams develop; establishing Student and Staff Support Teams at every school; building parent involvement programs system-wide; creating a full-time position to facilitate the change process; and developing a written curriculum that is aligned with district and state goals, responds to cultural differences and learning styles, and reflects a developmental perspective.

These elements reflect SDP's predilection—at least at the level of design theory—for defining the change process in structural terms. At the level of theory in use, however, SDP looks for more than a "yes" vote from a percentage of the community, and more than structural alignment. Valerie Maholmes, Director of the Teaching, Learning and Development Unit, told us that the success of a process that begins with the deliberations of a broad cross-section of a district's community is thought to hinge ultimately on whether the district is willing to implement the same process at the school level and to invest real power in it there. This is a political rather than merely structural criterion. Maholmes offered us a string of diagnostic questions on that score: "To what extent are the board and central office willing to support the devolving of some decisions that they typically make to the site level? Has that commitment been evidenced in any previous types of restructuring or plans to restructure? Is it evident in their strategic plan or their comprehensive district plan? Is it evident in the way they allocate funding to schools and who makes decisions about what, and things of that nature."

Ideally, Maholmes added, the result of what might be called SDP's initiation process is a district that is "ready to go." Meanwhile, the process is intended to make expectations clear on all sides, to make the choice to join or not join a clear-cut one, and—if the choice is to join—to ensure sufficient commitment and the necessary resources to guide implementation. Meanwhile, the process is designed to begin creating from the start of deliberations exactly the kind of organizational structure and culture that full implementation requires.

SYSTEMIC REFORM

Typically, the school reform strategy that often is called systemic reform proceeds by aligning curriculum, policies, assessments, training, and so on, toward a set of preferred and coherent student outcomes. The rallying cry is, What do we want all children to know and be able to do? At SDP, the rallying cry is subtly different: How can we encourage the development of all our children? (Comer, Haynes, Joyner, & Ben-Avie, 1996). One can imagine an answer to the former question that involves a set of standards plus some incentives and sanctions to use them. But the SDP question demands community reflection and community action, as well as the collaboration of all caregivers.

Jack Gillette and Robert Kranyik (1996) describe the experiential roots of SDP's systemic reform efforts as follows:

> We began to understand more and more about the district office's influence, both short-term and long-term, on the change process in schools. With the SDP process, local ownership becomes strengthened as the community connects and begins to gain a deeper understanding of its particular students. In enacting the child-centered process, schools not only can, but want to make instructional decisions for their buildings, and they spend their staff development resources accordingly. Such new operating processes inevitably conflict with standard operating practices, such as staff development initiatives, general district instructional directions, and the kind and quality of data collected and fed back to schools. (p.158)

To build on what it thus perceives as naturally occurring systemic interests, SDP has begun in recent years to work directly on systemic issues, agreeing, for example, to coach entire districts of schools. In doing so, it has sought to adapt the moves it has honed at the school level. All the assumptions at play in its work there are typically at play in this new arena too. One is the assumption that lack of coordination is the heart of the problem and, therefore, that coordination must be the heart of the solution. Another is that change requires facilitating structures—for example, district-wide mechanisms that correspond to the school-level mechanisms of the Comer Process. A third is that change requires patience. The result is that the SDP district-level work is on the conservative side of a continuum in reform perspectives on districts that runs on the other side to calls for dismantling them—as in advocacy for charter schools, voucher plans, and privatization schemes. The conservatism is not surprising given SDP's penchant for "staying in the middle," and given also a wider sense in the organization about the meaning of *systemic reform*. In James Comer's view, the *system* of interest goes far beyond what reformers typically mean by the term. "Schools are not the major problem," as he sees it, nor is the system of schooling in which they are enmeshed the major problem.

> The major problem is that we are a culture of individualism run amok, and a culture of exclusion to the point that we did not invest in most of the people after World War II. When the economy changed, the people we didn't invest in began to get into trouble. Instead of saying that we made policy errors, we began to blame it on people. The most vulnerable people in society, because of our peculiar history, were African Americans, and so we said as a society, it is not a societal problem, it is simply an African-American problem. . . . By scapegoating and blaming, we did not focus on problem solving . . . on the kind of health care we need, the kind of schools we need, the kind of child care we need, the kind of support for families, and development of communities that we need. (Comer, 1996, p. 3)

For nearly 30 years, Comer and his colleagues have chosen to work on this major *systemic* problem from the vantage point of schools and districts. But from this vantage point, they see schooling as symptomatic rather than causal. The distinction is important. For SDP, schooling is not a major causal factor in the decline of American prospects. The real cause lies elsewhere, as Comer suggests above, and this attitude has made him and SDP more cautious with respect to proposals to try to overhaul schools in some radically comprehensive way. To do that, they think, might be to engage in yet another scapegoating activity. A better way, they think, is to work on the problems of the American school in the larger context of engaging in community and youth development.

CHAPTER 3

The Coalition of Essential Schools in Its Second Decade

In October 1995, Sherry King addressed the staff at the national headquarters of the Coalition of Essential Schools at Brown University. A veteran of CES work as principal and superintendent, King spoke this day as chair of the Futures Committee. Formed a year earlier by Chairman and founder Ted Sizer to consider what CES might become in its second decade, the committee had just completed its report (Coalition of Essential Schools, 1995). King was reviewing a draft of it with the staff.

One of the report's findings was that the staff at Brown no longer had the capacity to support adequately what was becoming a huge network of schools—900 by then, more than 1,200 now. The report recommended that CES redefine its organizational structure and decentralize support of its schools. Rather than expect guidance from a professional staff at Brown, member schools should look to regional centers for assistance—leanly staffed operations with strong local roots. And CES should become a self-governing network of schools, led by a National Congress of representatives. King offered a familial explanation for her committee's report. "You see," she said, "the Coalition has grown up. We're leaving home. And by the way," she added, "we're taking with us some of what we like best: the Nine Common Principles, the Fall Forum, and [the publication] *Horace*."

The staff to whom she spoke that afternoon was already in transition as a result of the establishment at Brown of the Annenberg Institute for School Reform. With Ted Sizer as its first director, the Institute seemed at first a kind of permanently endowed organizational platform for the Coalition of Essential Schools. Yet, it soon had its own activities—particularly the $400 million Annenberg Challenge. Moreover, there was the insistence by Brown President Vartan Gregorian that the Institute be a "convenor" of multiple school reform efforts, not simply the home of the Coalition. Gradually, a crisis developed for CES and its veteran national staff. To which organization did they owe allegiance? Which Sizer was their boss—the one who was Director of the Institute or the one who was Chairman of CES? And which school reformers were their constituents: the diverse array of reformers who were emerging as the broad constituency of the Annenberg Institute, or the teachers and principals of CES schools with whom they had many close working relationships? Nor was the crisis merely about identity. In the face of the large Annenberg grant, funding for CES had begun to dry up. The jobs were now in the Institute, and, for a while, the momentum seemed to be there too. Meanwhile, the CES network of schools felt the same effects from its own perspective, and Sherry King's Futures Committee was convened in order to deal with them. In the process, it necessarily called attention to a question that seemed unnecessarily polar during the CES first decade. Was CES more a staff-based organization, or more an idea-based network of schools?

Eventually, the recommendations of the Futures Committee were adopted, and in due course most of the CES Brown staff either shifted to the Institute or else left Brown entirely. Among staff we interviewed for this chapter, many have since left CES. Meanwhile, Sizer stepped down from the directorship of the Institute to devote more time to CES, although not in an administrative capacity. Shortly thereafter, CES and the Annenberg Institute were formally separated, and CES became independent of Brown University, moving its central operations to Oakland, California. As former CES staff member Joe McDonald put it, "The network is becoming a network, after having lately been an overgrown school–university partnership." He thinks its only other choice would have been to become a university-based service organization, but this would not have squared well with its principles.

A PARADOXICAL IDENTITY

Long before the Futures Committee convened, CES was a network of schools voluntarily allied in school reform under the guidance of a common set of ideas articulated by Ted Sizer. Underlying these ideas is a school-centered theory of action, one that views school reform from the school up. Sizer himself has long evinced skepticism of what might be called professionally directed school reform or policy-directed school reform. One result is that CES-affiliated schools are independent in their reform activities and in their choice of advisors and consultants. In this respect, CES is quite different from SDP. On the other hand, as McDonald suggested, CES was *also* for much of its history a school–university partnership with a national professional staff led by Sizer at Brown University. In this respect, it was quite like SDP.

Until the transformation that began in 1995, therefore, CES was an organizational paradox. It was both a network of free-wheeling, reform-minded schools linked only by a set of common principles, and also a school reform "organization" led by professional facilitators, development specialists, researchers, and fund raisers. In its heyday, CES the organization was quite large and productive. Like its counterparts in the other ATLAS organizations, the CES central staff—as it called itself—developed many strategies and acquired and made many moves. These strategies and moves deeply affected CES the network—although they never quite defined it as in SDP.

To the question, "What are you?" Project Zero with relative clarity can answer: "We are a psychological research organization that recently has focused on applying our ideas to schooling." Education Development Center and the School Development Program can respond with similar definition albeit in different terms. But CES then and now must give a more complicated answer. It is an answer that the American school reform establishment repeatedly has failed to understand. The latter persists in categorizing CES exclusively as an organization-led school reform program, one with the traditional structure of outsiders working to implement changes on the inside of associated schools. Consider, for example, the frustration of researchers Sam Stringfield and Becki Herman (1994) in seeking to evaluate CES effectiveness by conventional means.

> Evaluating the Coalition would be much simpler if, for example, CES would state that, "By the end of five full years' participation in the Coalition, x percent of the . . . members of the Coalition will be awarding diplomas to students only upon demonstration of mastery."
>
> Evaluating the effects of membership in a "coalition" is not made easier when many of the strongest adherents of the group repeatedly stress that the Coalition "is not a *program*." (p. 20)

In CES, Stringfield and Herman obviously encountered something other than what they expected. Deborah Meier, co-founder of one of the first CES schools, as well as one of the most recent, and co-founder also of a network of them in New York City, has little sympathy for the researchers' plight. She told us that the idea of the Coalition as a reform organization working with schools doesn't make sense. The work of the Coalition is *in* schools and *among* schools, she said, and has little to do with people outside of those schools. Indeed, in one conversation with us, Meier challenged the premise of our book as one that looks at what outside reformers do to support inside reformers. "Spend your time in Coalition schools to understand the Coalition," she advised us. "Otherwise you're missing the point."

Indeed, of the five organizations we write about in this book, CES is the oddest fit with the book's focus and with the research methods underlying the book. Yet, it is incontrovertible that CES evolved into its current state not only as the result of considerable contributions from school-based CES leaders like Meier, but also as the result of the efforts of a staff at Brown University. During the CES first decade, this staff did help people inside schools, including Meier's school. It did design and conduct professional development programs. It did raise money for many CES schools. Moreover, it attempted to do all of these things on a national scale, in apparent contradiction of Sizer's belief that school change is a local endeavor best initiated and sustained by local schools and their communities. Members of the staff with whom we spoke acknowledged the paradox. To attempt to resolve it, they characterized their work not as permanent support but as temporary means to facilitate the growth and development of a young network. What we often heard in our meetings with the staff was that its role was to develop support moves, then "push them to a local level." Given such a strategy, Sherry King's October 1995 address to the CES staff does indeed seem pivotal. The network is ready now, she said in effect, to invent its own moves.

A PRINCIPLED USE OF PRINCIPLES

The Coalition of Essential Schools is based on ten Common Principles. The first nine are the product of a study of high schools that Sizer conducted in the early 1980s. The tenth was added by the CES Congress following the organizational transformation of 1995. With the exception of principle number nine, which is quite concrete (although also subject to much difference of interpretation), the principles are deliberately unspecific as well as highly provocative, even compelling. They invite experimentation and conversation about that experimentation. In our paraphrase, the Ten Common Principles are as follows:

1. The focus of school should be intellectual. The point is to teach students to use their minds well.
2. The school's goals should be simple: less is more.
3. The school's goals should apply universally to all students.
4. The school should be organized to know its students well and to personalize its teaching.

5. Teaching and learning should be organized so that students are active rather than passive learners. The governing metaphors of schooling should be student as worker, teacher as coach.
6. Graduation should be by exhibition. That is, the diploma should be awarded on the basis of a successful demonstration of the fact that the student has actually learned what the school set out to teach.
7. The tone of the school should be one of decency and of unanxious expectation.
8. Teachers should be generalists rather than specialists.
9. Teachers should have a total student load in secondary school of 80 or fewer students, and the costs of running a school on the basis of these principles should not rise more than 10% above what they are now.
10. The school should model democratic practices, honor diversity, and build on the strengths of its communities.

In 1985, Ted Sizer and his tiny staff did not envision that the experimentation and conversation based on these principles would take place among a Coalition of 1,200 Essential Schools. The initial CES theory of action had no clear commitment to CES growth. Rather, the implicit starting assumption was that Sizer and a start-up band of 12 schools would share the results of their experimentation with a country more or less ready to begin dismantling what Sizer's research colleague, Arthur Powell, had called the "shopping mall high school" (Powell, Farrar, & Cohen, 1985). Deborah Meier, whose Central Park East Secondary School signed on as one of the first "charter" schools of CES, recalled for us the start-up enthusiasm.

> We would stick with it, and try over 5 years to see how far we could push forward with the [then] Nine Common Principles. Ted believed that we could change the conversation about high schools. We could develop this small number of schools on a totally different basis, graduate kids in a different way. We could show others the possibilities, possibilities that would all be different: schools with different populations of kids, different political environments, coming up with different solutions.

CES was hardly a network then, and certainly not a school reform "organization" as described above. It was more a structured "conversation" among schools, each already working hard on reform by its own lights, but further inspired, encouraged—and, in a sense, protected—by Sizer and his ideas about school design. Sizer raised money that enabled the schools' principals to meet regularly. The money also enabled him to promote, in his writing and speaking engagements, the efforts the schools were making, of which there were many. In those days, one staff member told us, "Ted would go anywhere for the price of a cup of coffee if he thought it would help carry the conversation forward." The raised money also enabled him to develop a small staff to assist him in supporting the conversation. It was the latter that was to evolve into the CES staff at Brown. Yet, even after it had evolved into a staff some 30 members strong, and even as the voluntary participation of many schools in many corners of the United States and then abroad turned the conversation into a gigantic network, the determination abided in CES to stay conversational. This often has been expressed in the way that annoyed Stringfield and Herman, the researchers quoted above: "We're a conversation, not a program." It is a matter of principle at CES, and it has affected the development of strategy.

MULTIPLE CONVERSATIONS

In the beginning, with only 12 CES schools, all situated in the northeast, Sizer and his closest colleagues in reform—the schools' principals—were able to meet regularly, visit each other's schools, and get to know one another well. They shared experiences face to face and occasionally dared to challenge as well as learn from each other's approaches to the Common Principles. Moreover, they had little doubt *who* the Coalition of Essential Schools was—not Sizer's fledgling staff, but they themselves and their schools. Members of the CES staff told us that even years later, in the early 1990s, when the Coalition had grown to hundreds of schools, the "charter" schools network retained some of its early bonds. Although a few of the 12 schools were no longer intensely involved in CES work, their leaders still met regularly at the annual CES Fall Forum. The relationships endured.

Yet, by the time the network had grown beyond 50 or 75 or 100 schools, the kind of conversation common in the beginning had become problematic. New member schools were in many parts of the country, and because of geographical isolation, some worked more or less alone. On the other hand, there were some places where Essential schools seemed to beget other Essential schools, and where the resulting clusters used their proximity to engage in conversation like that of the original 12 schools. They became mini-networks and foreshadowed the emergence of the system of mini-networks that today constitutes the structure of the new CES. The early examples were in New York City, the San Francisco Bay

Area, Chicago, Broward County, Florida, Louisville, Kentucky, and a few other places. The key to starting and sustaining the local conversations was the intersection of strong leadership, good resources, and a commitment to build solidarity among the schools.

We asked Deborah Meier, who founded the CES mini-network in New York known as the Center for Collaborative Education, to describe the moves that may account for the Center's growth and achievement. The success, she told us, is a result of teachers who have directly experienced teaching in small, progressive, and democratically governed communities. Their experience secures their commitment to the ideas that underlie CES, and they teach both the ideas and the approaches that make them real to new colleagues and new schools. For Meier, this is what networking means: to teach commitment from a base of experience. "It's hard to do," she said, "if you haven't lived it. School change comes by building a school culture." To build that culture, she added, you need a small school, where everyone can know each other well, where trust and respect are mutual and universal among adults and students, and where the community democratically determines the norms and practices it will follow. A good school reform network, she thinks, builds a parallel culture from a parallel set of conditions.

Sizer told us that the New York network is successful because the people who make it up—in particular the principals of its schools—have the savvy to cope well with a complex, politically volatile environment where school people have to fight for resources and power every day. Their savvy is combined, he said, with aspects of the city itself that serendipitously serve to sustain a serious reform conversation. There is the subway system, for example, that allows students and teachers to travel easily to nearly any school in the city. There is the system of high-quality public colleges, like Hunter and City College, and private colleges also that collaborate with the network to develop appropriate resources for teachers in New York's alternative schools. There is a progressive teachers union sympathetic to alternative schools and a formal political leadership at the city and state level that intermittently has provided strong substantive and symbolic support to the city's alternative schools. "You don't find these things in L.A.," he added, "but you do in New York. Context is everything."

CES in its second decade seems very attuned to context and its capacity for stimulating and sustaining experimentation with and conversation about the Common Principles. Moreover, it is more resolute than ever in its sense that context cannot be imported as a program or manufactured absent the right local conditions. Today, the new CES Congress and Executive Board are especially attentive to the lessons they think they have learned from successful local CES conversations, such as those in New York.

Amy Gerstein, Executive Director of CES, told us that the new "member-driven" Coalition is built on a framework of mini-networks or "centers." The role of these centers, according to a recent memo of the organization's Executive Board, is to "work explicitly with CES schools to provide a forum for documenting, sharing, and publicly demonstrating their work." To do this well, the centers must be "of a size and scale that allow members to know each other well" (Coalition of Essential Schools, 1996). As of June 1997, there were 23 such centers in CES, as well as 23 additional smaller networks around the country, some of them only two or three schools big.

INVESTING IN SERENDIPITY

Almost from the beginning, there was another key dimension of the CES theory of action that seems paradoxical in combination with the dedication to sustained, intimate conversation. According to Ed Campbell, Executive Director of CES from 1988 to 1995, CES had to develop a strong national profile if its conversation was to be productive. "By 1988," Campbell told us, "people began to tell Ted that the Coalition had to be a lot bigger, and that if it didn't grow to be a lot bigger, it was going to be a drop in the bucket as far as the school reform movement was concerned." Many of these people were potential funders. Others were policy makers, who began in the late 1980s to become increasingly interested in school reform.

Heeding the warning, Sizer and his staff decided to go for breadth, even as they struggled to achieve some depth in the early member schools. Indeed, Sizer declared that simultaneous moves for breadth and depth are strategically essential and that they can be mutually supportive. He came to believe that he and his first colleagues had been naive to assume that 12 schools could obtain the degree of success necessary to demonstrate compelling alternative directions for school design. "You pick 12 schools," he told us, "and, given how difficult the work is, maybe two or three can pull it off successfully. But you don't convince the world with two or three schools. If you're only batting .200, you've got to start with a much larger number."

From the perspective of a programmatic orientation to school reform, Sizer's admission of "batting .200" might seem an admission of failure. But he and CES take it instead as an acknowledgment of the complexities involved. Their assumption is that programs, models, sets of principles, policy initiatives, money, great teachers, and the best of intentions will not *in and of themselves* ensure success in school change. This is because they are, by themselves, incapable of generating outstanding practice in schools. One can point to common elements among successful CES schools, Sizer told us, and these can be emulated. But just as important, he added, are the serendipitous elements: the right mix of people, timely policy breaks, local community receptivity, outstanding leadership. The .200 batting average reflects this circumstance and provokes an appropriate strategic response. With such a modest chance that any single school will achieve profound change, CES began after its first few years to encourage as many schools as possible to make the attempt and it equipped itself, as an organization, to invest in serendipity.

How can one invest in serendipity? Joe McDonald claims that chaos theory offers the basis for strategizing. In his book *Redesigning School* (1996), based on a study of 10 CES schools, he explains that serendipity may appear in any place at any time—although, predictably, it will continually appear somewhere. The strategic trick, he argues, is to remain organizationally nimble enough to shift resources as needed in order to support it wherever it appears, and to get out quickly whenever prospects drop. "This is not the view of change that rationalists prefer," he told us, "but it explains why some reformers try to create movements rather than rational schemes."

McDonald spoke of the Coalition as a "big tent," the school reform equivalent of the revival tents that once inspired the small towns of late-nineteenth-century America each summer. This big tent, he said, preaches a particular set of beliefs, the Ten Common Principles. The beliefs are broad ones, not dogmatic, and are meant to be interpreted and customized. All schools are welcome within the tent. And all schools are represented in the tent: rich, poor, private, public, parochial, White, Black, big, small. Once inside, these schools are encouraged to be themselves and to develop as each sees fit, provided each makes a fair effort to abide by the principles that attracted them to it in the first place. Once inside, a school can expect to be supported, encouraged, and respected by fellow schools, even though the direction it takes may be different from the directions of its colleagues. Each school is free to enter the tent, free to determine its own destiny, free to succeed and free to fail. And always free to leave. But the movement is always on the lookout for schools that seem to be succeeding. These "offer witness" to the others and are rewarded with extra support.

McDonald believes that changing schools is such an overwhelming task that schools and people in them need the support of a power bigger than themselves. In the case of CES, the "power" is a combination of the Common Principles and the collective belief they inspire. "CES is an affiliation, an interest group that crosses regional and political jurisdictions," he told us, "that provides its members support quite apart from the efforts of anyone sitting in Providence or in any regional office." His statement emphasizes CES the network. He describes a school reform initiative quite different in approach from those that emphasize systemic policy change or fidelity to imported programs. In his characterization, CES is fundamentally the movement of a group of schools with a common inspiration. "Low-church school reform," he calls it. In contrast to high-church school reform that emphasizes the application of doctrine, low-church reform in his characterization emphasizes the application of belief.

What moves are associated with low-church school reform? Two are especially important. First, there is the big tent itself, which in the case of the Coalition of Essential Schools is the annual Fall Forum. Second, there are the texts that bind the community and that keep the conversation going even when the tent is down. We'll look at each of these substrategies in turn.

The Fall Forum, a yearly gathering of the network, embodies on a national scale what Ted Sizer often describes as the fundamental nature of the Coalition, namely, "a conversation among friends." As we mentioned earlier, the CES network of the mid-1980s was literally an intimate conversation among friends, one that took place at periodic meetings of the leaders of the first schools. These meetings offered them opportunities to share their experiences and provide one another practical and moral support.

As CES began to grow, Sizer and his staff designed bigger meetings that were open also to those interested in becoming affiliated. After a series of regional meetings of this sort in 1987 and 1988, the staff decided to hold a grand meeting, a national gathering that could accommodate as many interested people as possible from all over the country. The result was the first Fall Forum, held in Providence in 1988. Amy Gerstein, who helped plan that gathering, recalled that she and her colleagues anticipated 200 to 400 participants. Four hundred and fifty showed up. Thereafter, the turnout nearly doubled each year, until the Coalition decided to cap participation at 4,000, where it stands today. Since its inception, the Fall Forum has assumed a powerful presence within the network. Some within the Coalition community describe it with almost religious fervor, regarding it as a yearly opportunity to renew one's commitment to the work of reform. Others see it in more political terms, a chance to develop new relationships and broaden one's network and base of support. In speaking with us, Gerstein acknowledged the validity of both these images and also added a third. She compared the Fall Forum with an intense, and intensely positive, family reunion. The first Fall Forum, she said, provided such collective inspiration to the participants that it took the staff by surprise.

Part of the value of the Fall Forum to the network, according to Gerstein, is that it seems to enact CES principles. So, for example, participants reflect the entire education system, from teachers and parents to researchers and state commissioners of education; but in contrast to other education conferences, she said, the Fall Forum is not hierarchical: Teachers speak on a par with school superintendents, parents with researchers. If there is any deference at all for position at the Fall Forum, she added, it may be for teachers. "Teachers," she said, "are the champions. There is a sense that everyone at the Fall Forum is working hard at reform, but that teachers are working the hardest."

Like CES more broadly, the Fall Forum is a collaborative undertaking. Although Brown-based staff still contribute crucial coordination, the bulk of the planning and program development are made by a large and regionally dispersed committee. Teachers and principals, regional facilitators, and what Gerstein called other "friends in the conversation" submit proposals to fill 2- or 3-hour program slots. "You have to have a long block to do anything serious," Gerstein told us. The proposals are reviewed by dozens of peer judges across the country, who make the final choices. Moreover, on site, the Fall Forum's pedagogy is interactive. Workshops enact the principle of "student as worker/teacher as coach." In addition to workshops, "Roundtables" offer participants opportunities to converse in some depth about a particular school's work. According to Gerstein, the expertise at a Fall Forum is considered to reside in the participants themselves, and this is perhaps nowhere more evident than in these lively Roundtables.

A second "low-church" move mentioned above—one that keeps the conversation going between Fall Forums—involves the publication of texts. Two different kinds of texts have proved invaluable to the CES network—as, indeed, to many others involved in school reform who have read them. The first set are Ted Sizer's own writings. In *Horace's Compromise* (1984), *Horace's School* (1992a), and most recently *Horace's Hope* (1996)—as well as in countless formal and informal letters to CES principals and friends over the years—Sizer has tried to keep the conversation going, and to keep it both focused and fresh. At the same time, he also has sought to initiate diverse newcomers to the conversation. He told us that friends in the academic publishing community urged him to go straight to a trade publisher when he finished his first draft of what was to become *Horace's Compromise*. They convinced him that the work would have influence only if the widest possible public had access to it. But Sizer previously had written for university audiences only. He told us how his trade editor reacted to the draft, which was heavily academic. "I love it," the editor said, "now rewrite it." The end result of what Sizer called a "savage" editing process was that his ideas, now cast for a broader audience, were claimed immediately by a large one.

A second set of key CES texts is the extraordinary collection of brief monographs on various topics associated with the Common Principles that have been written since 1988 by Kathleen Cushman in the periodical *Horace*. It began as an informal newsletter of the Coalition, a bulletin board for sharing information, raising questions, and generally keeping member schools informed about the network's progress. By 1988, Ted Sizer began to see copies of this early version of *Horace* in important places, like the desks of foundation officers or the hands of influential policy makers and leaders in education. His response might well have been to turn *Horace* the bulletin board into *Horace* the public relations mouthpiece of the Coalition. He decided instead on a different transformation. He decided to go for greater depth in *Horace*, to use it as a means of exploring CES ideas and practices with all the complexities and tensions acknowledged, to make it in effect a major input to the conversation. He figured that foundation officers, policy makers, and others who also might read it would be wiser for having read serious treatments of serious issues.

To this end, he recruited a writer, Cushman, whose work he knew and admired, and he asked her to explore Essential schooling with a kind of tough-minded sympathy. She told us that she made it clear to him that she "would not write PR," and he made it clear to her that he didn't want PR. He wanted each issue of *Horace* to address in depth a single important dimension of school reform in the spirit of CES—to explore the ideas and practices associated with it within the larger conversation. She promised issues of roughly 4,500 words and entered into a contract with him at her regular freelance magazine rate for five issues a year. Her first issue came out in September 1988, and she has written every *Horace* since.

When she began, Cushman had no professional experience in education. What she did have was experience as a writer and as a parent—a parent concerned about the school experiences of her children and frustrated by her limited success in effecting change in their schools. But with Sizer's approbation, she took her rookie status in education to be an asset—she could avoid being either too familiar or too skeptical. Her early credentials, she told us, were those of a "naïve questioner." She began to generate ideas for issues with the help of members of the CES staff at Brown. Susan Fisher, then CES Director of Publications and now in the same role at the Annenberg Institute, served as liaison to the network and as editor. Fisher was uniquely positioned to know what topics were most pressing among CES schools. She fielded daily requests from schools looking for help on a range of difficult questions. Through Fisher's "assignments," Cushman was able to tune her writing to real concerns in the network. The result was a string of influential issues—on exhibitions, scheduling, advisory systems, documenting school progress, examining student work, and many others.

With Fisher gone now, and a much leaner Brown staff in place, Cushman depends for her topics more directly on the network itself, using electronic mail to stay in touch with a large number of the network's people. Meanwhile, 9 years and nearly 50 issues later, she is hardly any longer the naïve questioner. "My approach is more educated now," she told us, "and this is both an asset and a liability—asset that I know more things, liability that I might get stale or jargonistic."

We asked Cushman about the moves she employs to produce a typical *Horace*. She told us that once she has decided on a topic—having vetted the choice through the network—she uses e-mail and telephone "to cast the net as widely as possible," to find the people inside and outside the network who know the most about the topic. She described her process as a cross between essay writing and journalism. It is essay writing in the sense that she tries to capture the complexity and tensions within a given issue. It is journalism in that she employs the techniques of a reporter to get as many pertinent perspectives on an issue as possible and searches out contrary voices to get the fullest picture. Thus, she said, when individuals or factions within the network challenge a particular issue's slant, or criticize Cushman for not addressing certain topics, she goes straight to the challengers and asks, "What should I be writing about? Who should I be interviewing?" The result, she says, is a format that attempts to reflect the best knowledge available on a given issue and depicts the different, often conflicting perspectives on that issue.

Cushman believes that in an effort like CES, something like *Horace* is crucial. Its mission, she told us, is simple on the surface: "Put into clear language the ideas of the Coalition and how they look when you do them." But there is a deep rationale. She believes that "all ideas are based on images. A program or recipe is absolutely the wrong way to make social change," she told us. "The only way to spread ideas is through concrete images and letting these ideas and images talk to each other." That is what every good essay does, she says, and why she likes to say that in writing *Horace* she is as much essayist as journalist. She thinks, moreover, that in this respect, *Horace* merely exemplifies the discourse that can and should be the basis of work in CES schools and centers.

THE STRATEGIES DISCUSSED ABOVE—involving the launching and support of intimate conversation about the Common Principles, and the reliance on regionalization as well as movement methods for broadening and sustaining the conversation—are as characteristic of CES today as at any moment in its past. Several other key CES strategies, however, have been left behind in the new effort to emphasize the network over the organization. We examine them here, nonetheless, because one cannot otherwise understand what CES has become and why.

SYSTEMIC REFORM

To avoid being what Ed Campbell called a "drop-in-the-bucket" school reform effort, the CES national staff decided in 1988 to grow CES into a major national network by means of a strategic alliance with the Education Commission of the States (ECS). The partners were aided in this effort by major grants from the Carnegie Corporation and from an anonymous benefactor. ECS had been working with state governments since the 1960s to shape state education policies and was interested in the late 1980s in helping states plan and carry out thoughtful school reform initiatives. It had the national reach that CES lacked and access to state resources. For its part, CES brought school-level experience in school reform to the partnership, as well as Sizer's charisma and the strength of his ideas. Under the banner *Re:Learning: From Schoolhouse to Statehouse*, ECS and CES encouraged individual states to commit resources to existing or prospective Essential schools and to develop policy environments that favored their experimentation with and conversation about the Nine Common Principles. Typically, the latter took the form of policy waivers rather than policy changes. Ed Campbell, who joined CES early in 1990, described the Re:Learning strategy as part marketing and part systemic support. The idea was to "open up a market" for CES development in new places, and at the same time help ensure supportive contexts for this development. From a policy perspective, the Re:Learning initiative invited states to reconsider their traditional attitude toward schools, to begin to think of them as generators of new policy rather than merely implementers of it. This was the meaning of the initiative's slogan, Schoolhouse to Statehouse. Although it lacked the comprehensiveness of later initiatives that appropriated the term, this was one of the earliest efforts at creating *systemic reform*—that is, reform that aims at the contexts affecting schools as well as schools themselves.

Each Re:Learning state was required to appoint a Re:Learning coordinator from its own ranks, who then would work with the support of one CES staff person and one ECS staff person. During the early Re:Learning days, Beverly Simpson was one of the small staff of CES "gardeners" who represented CES in Re:Learning and who worked directly with state coordinators to help manage the partnership. The garden metaphor was one of three horticultural ones that CES in those days used to define the different roles of its central staff. The garden referred to Re:Learning and other school outreach efforts in the field; the toolshed to such activities as fund raising, publications, and financial management; and the hothouse to research and development. The nature of a gardener's work, Simpson told us (adding still other metaphors), was "part cultivator, part missionary, part sales force." She also felt sometimes like an "itinerant storyteller," traveling to schools and groups of schools that had expressed interest in becoming members of CES. She would introduce schools to the Common Principles, ask questions, provide schools with feedback, but make a conscious effort throughout her visits not to play the role of a consultant or expert. Her role, instead, she said, was to facilitate a school's conversation about itself and its goals without defining or pushing the conversation in a prescribed way.

Even in the early stages of the Re:Learning work, the numbers of schools signing on for various stages of CES membership grew so quickly that Simpson and her "garden" colleagues, as well as their ECS and state counterparts, were nearly overwhelmed. Eventually, the gardeners decided to work less directly with schools and spend more time providing support to the state coordinators. The approach yielded mixed results. Where state coordinators were sufficiently entrepreneurial and enjoyed good support from their states, Re:Learning was able to assist new CES schools fairly well. In other cases, they were not.

Of course, the Re:Learning strategy was highly susceptible to shifts in state politics, and according to both Ted Sizer and Ed Campbell, CES had underestimated the fickle nature of these politics. Sizer believes that he and his colleagues, including the governors themselves, were naïve not to see that even very promising short-term accomplishments at the state level inevitably would be altered, undermined, or abandoned as political climates changed, as governors left office, and as political commitments to education moved elsewhere. Of the five initial governors who gave the greatest push to Re:Learning at its inception in 1988, most were out of office within 5 years. Key legislators, once committed, often withdrew support or shifted their support to other initiatives. In the climate of what many policy analysts call "policy churn," Re:Learning stood little chance of having any substantial impact on state policy. Certainly the dream of orienting policy "from schoolhouse to statehouse" was achieved nowhere. Despite the best efforts of Re:Learning, as Ed Campbell put it, "most state departments of education still think they're actually the ones who determine what happens out there in the schools."

The intended irony of his remark reveals a deep-seated belief at CES— one even stronger now for its experience with Re:Learning. Simply put, it is that American schools—for better or worse—function independently of most external attempts to regulate them, whether by states or districts. A corollary assumption is that to affect schools in any serious way, and especially to ensure that they teach all children well, one must do more than regulate: One must find a way to affect their prevailing beliefs.

Whatever its failings as a policy initiative in the ordinary sense, the Re:Learning initiative significantly spurred the growth and the geographical spread of CES membership. The commitment of Re:Learning governors to waive regulations for CES schools and to encourage CES membership created what Sizer called "a surge" of schools toward CES. One consequence of the surge was elevated awareness of CES nationally and of its message of school-centered school reform. Moreover, as other "systemic initiatives" succeeded Re:Learning in the states, CES often used its new clout—both locally and nationally—to press them to take schools seriously as the necessary agents of their own reform and to treat schools, in Joe McDonald's phrase, "as systems in their own right, not just the nodes of one." Sizer, more than any other figure in contemporary school reform, has championed this school-sensitive view, and in an important sense, Re:Learning gave him the platform.

At the same time, the Re:Learning surge of new CES schools had another important strategic impact on CES. As Bev Simpson put it, the breadth of the initiative overwhelmed any effort by the central staff to work directly with schools in order to help achieve depth. Even the state Re:Learning coordinators were unable to work in a sustained way with individual schools. The experience helped turn CES away from the tendency of its middle years to be a school reform "organization"—that is, an external provider of reform expertise. It forced CES to consider other means of spreading the Common Principles.

Given the mixed results of Re:Learning, we asked Ted Sizer to consider with the benefit of hindsight how else CES might have used the funds and energies it expended on the initiative. He told us that it should have looked less to public policy as a spur and more to local communities committed to starting new schools, particularly ones that seemed to have the local political support necessary to reduce the threat of reform backlash. "I would have figured out how to be more radical than we were being," he said. "The Coalition schools that have moved most rapidly are new schools: Central Park East Secondary School [New York], Salem High School [Georgia], Souhegan [New Hampshire], University Heights [New York], Sedona Red Rock [Arizona]. These are very different schools from the average American high school. I should have raised a big slug of money and then wandered around the country and found those places where there was need for new schools like these, and communities that wanted them. The Coalition's reputation has been disproportionately carried by new schools that didn't have to fight rearguard action every time they wanted to change something."

A NATIONAL FACULTY

Re:Learning is especially responsible for making CES a national effort, and the initiative known as the National Re:Learning Faculty is especially responsible for making it a genuine network. Perhaps more than any other factor, it is responsible for ensuring that CES never became an utterly staff-dominated organization.

Beginning in the late 1980s, alongside the Re:Learning initiative, the CES staff initiated several professional development strategies. For example, the Trek program led teams of teachers from Coalition schools through an extensive year-long planning process designed to help schools manage the change process. In other programs, staff conducted national and regional workshops addressing aspects of the Common Principles. However inventive in other respects, these activities were conventional in one important respect: They were offered by schooling's outsiders for the benefit of its insiders. The National Re:Learning Faculty offered another idea.

The Faculty got its members from two programs. One was the Thompson Fellows Program, originally funded by the Danforth Foundation. This program selected principals from various CES schools and brought them together periodically over the course of 2 years to have the same kind of conversation that the principals of the original 12 CES schools had in the early CES years. It also encouraged and supported consulting efforts by these principals (and, for a time, by a small group of superintendents as well).

The second program grooming members of the National Re:Learning Faculty was the Citibank Fellows Program, funded by a grant from Citibank Corporation. This program brought selected teachers from CES schools together for a summer of intense collaborative teaching and learning experiences. The teachers taught together in a special summer school originally designed to provide Brown University teacher education students their first practice teaching. For many of the Citibank Fellows, it provided their first experience in team teaching, or in teaching interdisciplinary curriculum, or in teaching like a coach, or in using exhibitions. According to Paula Evans, founder and co-director of the program (as well as of the larger Re:Learning Faculty effort), the program assumed that even excellent teachers need transformational teaching experiences. "It isn't enough," she wrote in 1994, "to come together and have a good talk.

. . . Many teachers and principals have not experienced themselves what it means to be pushed intellectually, to exhibit knowledge publicly, to generate knowledge" (p. 44).

Citibank Fellows Camilla Greene and Ted Hall—she an English teacher, he a science teacher—taught together in the Brown Summer High School. Thoughtful and experienced teachers already, they used their experience together to perform an experiment—one they would have found difficult to perform by themselves in the contexts of their regular classrooms. They tried to make their 4-week course as "student-centered" and as "de-teacherized" as possible. Greene told us, "Ted and I gave each other the courage to say, 'Let's see what happens if we don't front-load all of the information,' and we began to look at what was the minimum amount of direction that we could give to kids to move them to produce something. And it worked for students. We saw more engagement."

The first purpose of the Citibank Fellows' experience then was to deepen their knowledge of and commitment to the Common Principles—and by means of two standard CES tools: experimentation and conversation. The second purpose, however, was to train the Citibank teachers to be consultants too. In addition to tending to their own development as teachers during their Citibank summer, these Fellows were expected also to reflect on how the challenges in their own learning might be said to exemplify those involved in school reform generally. Each interdisciplinary teaching team frequently was visited by other teams in their classrooms, and the observers and observed engaged in pre- and postteaching conversations about teaching and learning and schooling. These conversations provided the context for their training as consultants. Like most American teachers, they were unused to collaboration and unused also to talking with other teachers about teaching and schooling. The program acknowledged this learning gap and tried to fill it, while keeping the participants' attention aggressively focused on what Evans calls "looking at practice."

Herself a former teacher, Paula Evans explained to us that the Citibank project was based on three assumptions. The first was the belief that the most important object of reform is teacher practice—rather than, say, policy or school structure. The second was that the new CES consultants—being themselves teachers—had an advantage in the effort to affect their peers and that they would have instant credibility among their peers. The third assumption was that the only kind of consultation for school change worth the time or expense is the kind that is sustained over time. Thus the Citibank Fellows were trained not as one-shot consultants (much to the chagrin of some CES staff, reeling under the Re:Learning load, and hoping for a little relief), but rather as long-term consultants.

Evans acknowledged to us that these assumptions cut against the grain of most school improvement efforts, dominated as they tend to be by outside experts and one-shot inservice workshops. Indeed, the idea of a teacher as a long-term consultant for change is so unusual that, after the initial cohort of Citibank Fellows had completed the first summer program, there was very little demand for their services. As Evans put it, they were "all dressed up with no place to go."

The demand rose thereafter, however, partly as the result of prodding by Evans and her colleague Gene Thompson-Grove. Eventually, many Citibank Fellows did some consulting work, and some developed significant practices as school reform consultants. A few, like Camilla Greene and Ted Hall, even became CES staff members. The largest impact of the Citibank program, however, was indirect. It spread what might be called an authoritative sense of CES expertise beyond the Brown-based staff and it also spread allegiance to the CES network beyond CES school principals.

These effects were not without controversy, though. Some principals and some CES staff felt that the special allegiance to CES created by the Citibank training, as well as the call that some Fellows experienced to share their new expertise with other schools, cut the Fellows off from their own schools, effectively robbing the schools of a precious resource. In the long run, however, according to Evans, the Citibank Fellows enriched the network as a whole, and this has benefited all the schools within it.

RESEARCH AND DEVELOPMENT

CES began as a response to the findings of a research project, Sizer's early 1980s inquiry into the failings of the American high school. The first 12 schools used these findings as important, although hardly sufficient, input to their reform work. The assumption then was that research findings need the complementary findings of experimentation and conversation. Throughout the first decade of CES, research continued to play an important role within the organization and across the network, and typically in this same dialectical relationship with experimentation and conversation. The first CES researcher was Grant Wiggins, whose inquiries into curriculum, assessment, and pedagogy had an enormous impact on the development of CES practices. Later CES researchers, working in the same R&D fashion, included Rick Lear, Pat Wasley, Joe McDonald, David Niguidula, and David Allen.

Some of these same researchers—joined by external researchers Donna Muncey and Patrick McQuillan—also participated in a multiproject, decade-long effort to document the work of schools seeking to redesign themselves by the light of the Common Principles. The most important products of this effort are Muncey and McQuillan's (1996) report of an ethnography of some CES pioneer schools, McDonald's reports from the Exhibitions Project (McDonald, 1996; McDonald, Smith, Turner, Finney, & Barton, 1993), and Wasley's reports from the Teacher Change and School Change Projects (Wasley, 1995; Wasley, Hampel, & Clark, 1997a). The cumulative effort represented in these publications marked CES in its first decade as a research-minded organization, although the research itself and its relationship to the practice of reform differ in character from the kind of research undertaken by more program-focused school reform efforts, including SDP. That is, although CES has raised millions to document the reform efforts of its schools, it has never sponsored research to "test" its programmatic effectiveness. That is because, as the reader may recall, CES has never regarded itself as a testable program.

Pat Wasley's work especially exemplifies CES research. As a CES senior researcher, she led major inquiries into the complex and difficult work of serious school change. Rejecting ordinary social science efforts to achieve distance and objectivity in her research efforts, Wasley used methods designed to combine validity with empathy and support.

For example, the School Change Study, undertaken by Wasley together with colleagues Robert Hampel and Richard Clark, was designed from the beginning with the help of the participant schools. The goals, subjects, methods of inquiry, and prospective products of the research were all "negotiated." The point of the negotiation, according to Wasley, was to ensure that the project served the developmental needs of both the schools and the larger network. As the director of the research, she represented the interests of the latter as she saw them—the need to take a close and unflinching look at the progress of five seriously reform-minded high schools. The schools were enlisted in the project because they showed early promise, but CES was accustomed by then to the fickle quality of early promise and needed to protect its right to the whole story. For their part, the schools—represented by their principals in the negotiation—had to protect their right to learn from the research in progress—in effect, to ensure that a research effort was also a development effort. Trying to satisfy both these interests, according to Wasley, strengthens both school change efforts and research about them.

Two "negotiated" aspects of the School Change Study are particularly worth noting here. The first was the decision to focus on the impact of change on students—to use their experiences as a medium for understanding reform. Thus the project attempted to fill an important gap in research on school reform, namely, the gap in understanding reform as a process in the lives of students rather than merely an invisible means of producing what are called "student outcomes." For 3 years, Wasley and her colleagues followed the same students, observing them in classes and interviewing them in focus groups, seeing their schools' progress—or lack of progress—through their eyes. At the same time, the researchers aimed to fill another gap, this time on the development side. The schools in their study, like nearly every other American high school, lacked mechanisms for studying in any complex and longitudinal way their impact on their own students. Like nearly every other reform-minded school, they also lacked a reliable means of knowing how their students felt about changes underway in their school.

A second fruit of the negotiations that preceded the School Change Study was the development of a method of inquiry that the researchers and schools came to call "the snapshot." Three times a year for 3 years, Wasley's team visited each study school and collected data. Following each of these visits, the researchers prepared written "snapshots" of the school based on these data. As Wasley put it, the snapshots attempted to capture "what was going on, what the issues were, what kids were saying, what adults were saying, what parents were saying." The team mailed each full snapshot to the school's faculty and sent relevant sections to students and parents as well; and they invited all readers to return written comments. After these were returned, the researchers visited the schools again to discuss the snapshots at faculty meetings. The purpose of these activities was to provide schools an otherwise unattainable glimpse of their own operations in progress, and in the process to help them see the gap, if any, between what they say they want to do and what they actually do (King, Louth, & Wasley, 1993). But the researchers also did more than this. They provided the schools the opportunity to dispute what the snapshots implied, to discuss these implications, and, over time, to build school-level capacity for reflective action. The latter was the special fruit of the project, in Wasley's view, although it did not grow in every school. Receiving such feedback as Wasley and her colleagues offered is not easy—even for reform-minded schools. However, those schools that tolerated the enormous initial discomfort, Wasley told us—and that took advantage of the researchers' efforts to help them deal with this discomfort—evolved significantly in what might be called their organizational capacity for learning. Other schools remained more reticent, however, less willing to look at the data squarely, more willing to deflect the feedback, and ultimately unsuccessful in putting it to use.

Wasley and her colleagues' work has been published in multiple formats, including case studies designed as texts for discussion by other schools in the CES network, an article about whole-school change (Wasley, Hampel, & Clark, 1997b), and a book called *Kids and School Reform* (Wasley,

Hampel, & Clark, 1997a). The researchers also have written and spoken about the ways in which their experimental methods might contribute to others' efforts to redefine the roles of researchers and other "outsiders" in school reform (Wasley, King, & Louth, 1995). But perhaps the most important impact of their work on CES—and, indeed, the most important impact of the CES research done by Muncey, McQuillan, and McDonald—has been in helping the schools of the network appreciate the complexities and tortuous qualities of serious whole-school change. Wasley told us that she hopes her work persuades some CES schools to set aside the ordinary tendency of schools to think that "planning for tomorrow is much more powerful than examining what happened today, yesterday, historically." As CES embarks on what its new Congress has proclaimed a "decade of demonstration," the network will need many schools that have learned this "Essential Lesson."

CHAPTER 4

Project Zero as School Reformer

In many ways, Project Zero's Development Group became a school reformer by accident. Unlike the School Development Program and the Coalition of Essential Schools, it did not begin with a reform vision, then build a set of strategies to put the vision into place. It began instead with a research program that was originally unconcerned with reform. However, certain of the findings of this research program happened to stimulate an interest in reform, and certain of its orientations and habits happened to steer that interest toward a particular theory of action. By degrees, PZ became a reformer, and oddly enough one whose theory of action resembles in certain important ways those of the organizations that became its ATLAS partners. We say "oddly enough" because PZ's strategies and moves as school reformer owe at least as much to research traditions as to the traditions of activist reform that have tended to be the main influence on its partners. And we say "oddly enough" also because most research traditions regard practice merely as an application site, although PZ clearly does not.

Until the early 1980s, PZ was involved in what Howard Gardner once called "pure research—philosophical and psychological research." This research often focused on schoolchildren, but with an emphasis on the *children* not the *school*. Gardner once whimsically referred to PZ's work in schools prior to 1980 as plucking children out of class, giving them a 10-minute task, then sending them back with a handful of M & Ms. The tasks these children engaged in over the years, however, contributed to a body of data that eventually would challenge Jean Piaget's conception of development and contribute to Gardner's theory of multiple intelligence. And it was this theory that especially led Gardner and his colleagues into much closer collaboration with schools and school reform. Today, PZ's approach to school reform encompasses several efforts to generate research-based ideas about cognitive development and—rather than "apply" them—to give them what PZ calls "a push into school practice."

It was largely the response to *Frames of Mind* (Gardner, 1983)—in which Multiple Intelligences (MI) theory was outlined—that took Project Zero on the path of becoming a school reformer. As we recounted in Chapter 1, Howard Gardner had not anticipated teachers' intense interest in MI and had not had them in mind as audience for the book. But once teachers began to respond so enthusiastically, he understood the connection. The theory found acceptance among many teachers, he surmised, because it reflected their practical experiences in the classroom and their intuitive understanding of development built on years of teaching. "Anybody who has contact with lots of kids," Gardner told us, "knows that they're not all the same. And particularly if they have students with learning problems, they know that doesn't mean the students are stupid. The theory matched people's intuitions."

Spurred on by the strong response to MI, Project Zero has de-emphasized its role in "pure" research and taken on more of an activist approach. As we suggested above, however, PZ has not turned to "applied research" of the conventional sort, whereby schools may be viewed as mere adopters of research-generated ideas and techniques. PZ has instead defined its activist stance with greater subtlety and greater respect for the cultures of practice and the knowledge of teachers. As PZ researcher Noel White told us, PZ looks at schools and classrooms as "places we can learn from" rather than merely contribute to. Thus in many projects over the past 15 years, PZ researchers have used research perspectives and theories of human development to learn more about learning in the contexts of actual schools and with teachers as partners. At the same time, they have sought to contribute to the further development of these teachers' practices. It is often difficult to know—when one looks at a particular project of this sort—which purpose came first, the researcher's or the reformer's. In fact, in most cases, the question is academic, since the two perspectives tend to intermingle early.

Very recently too, PZ has expanded its school reform work, beyond the contexts of classrooms and partnerships with particular teachers, to include some projects that seek to foster whole-school change. ATLAS itself is one such example.

A COMMITMENT TO THE ARTS, THE MIND, AND LEARNING

Project Zero's theory of action guiding its work as school reformer owes much to its roots as an organization founded to explore the arts and human cognition. From the beginning of its work in the late 1960s, PZ has sought to understand development in the arts from a rational perspective, an approach that historically had been ignored and even denigrated. A rational approach to the arts bucked the prevailing trend in Western thought that tagged the arts as "antirational" and sought to confine arts learning exclusively to the emotional and spiritual realms, and in the process to discount its importance.

Later, as PZ undertook efforts to study learning in the other disciplines also, it brought a determination—honed in its arts-related work—to avoid narrow conceptions of learning and cognition. This became a matter of principle. "We don't just focus on problem solving or basic skills," Tina Blythe told us, a former teacher and long-time research associate at PZ. "We focus on what really matters when you get outside of school and want to become an expert in something." From a PZ perspective, the goal is "high end" or "deep" understanding. This is defined as the kind of understanding that is needed to succeed in any profession and that characterizes exceptional performance in domains that range from music to interpersonal relations.

A second principle in PZ's theory of action involves interest in the individual human mind. More than with the other ATLAS partners, the individual is central at PZ. From the distinctive contributions of accomplished artists to the multiple intelligences of children, PZ tries to understand and respond to individual differences. At first glance, a commitment to individual differences hardly seems radical; we all can readily recognize and appreciate differences among individuals. Yet in the context of an education system that often treats students as interchangeable in some respects, and different only in gross ways—smart and not-so-smart, college-bound or otherwise—the invitation to consider and act on individual difference is a huge challenge to ordinary practice. As a matter of espoused theory, PZ asks of itself and of school people: "If we take differences among individuals seriously, what does that mean for education?" As Howard Gardner puts it, "I have always believed that the heart of the MI perspective—in theory and in practice—inheres in taking seriously the differences among human beings. At the theoretical level, one acknowledges that all individuals cannot be arrayed on a single intellectual dimension. At the practical level . . . any uniform educational approach is likely to serve only a minority of children" (Gardner, 1995).

Finally, a third PZ principle involves a commitment to learning that resists the kind of closure common in most learning ventures. As one PZ staff member told us, "PZ almost never says it has an answer, and, on the rare occasion that it does, it uses the answer less as an end in itself and more as an opening to a new round of questions." Continuous learning is, in some sense, always and everywhere the basic mission of the organization. As in its initial commission to "learn something about education in the arts," PZ's projects are committed invariably to studying deeply and to generating new ideas. However, in recent years, this commitment has edged away from the traditional academic notion of "contributing to theoretical knowledge" as a thing apart from practical work in the field of human development. Today, the effort to learn continuously at PZ is tied more often to actual learning contexts, although not just schools. It is important to note here that while this chapter portrays PZ's work with schools, several of its projects (not portrayed) are partnerships with other kinds of learning institutions, from community arts centers to drama institutes and museums.

In whatever learning contexts it studies, PZ's efforts to understand and to promote learning have been deeply influenced by these three principles. As school reformer, for example, it is more radical in its vision and more suspicious of quick solutions because of its history of avoiding narrow definitions of cognition, of promoting deep understanding, and of searching for school designs that genuinely respect the individuality of children's minds. And it is more respectful of the cultures of schools and of the knowledge of teachers because of its habit of avoiding closure in learning opportunities and of eschewing presumptions that it has answers for the problems of schools.

While they have inspired PZ's strategies as school reformer, the three principles also have created tensions in that work. PZ staff members have had to learn ways to balance the demands of a continuous learning agenda with the demands of partner teachers and schools for some degree of closure. They have had to develop approaches that support "deep learning" without denying the responsibilities of schools to support other kinds of learning too. And they have had to learn to accommodate their interest in individual development, however uneasily, to the structural and cultural norms of schooling that emphasize group learning and that often unduly constrain individual development (whether of students or of teachers).

A "PROJECT-BASED" ORGANIZATION

PZ staff talked to us about a variety of school-based projects they have managed since 1983 and of their practice as research-based reformers. These projects include Project Spectrum, focused on helping students develop and demonstrate a wide range of cognitive capacities; the APPLE project (Assessing Projects and Portfolios for Learning), designed to help teachers incorporate portfolios and project-based curricula in their teaching; the After School Project, focused also on curriculum development; and the Teaching for Understanding Project, focused on producing a curriculum framework and techniques to help students achieve a deep understanding of critical concepts in a variety of disciplines.

Organized like its ATLAS partner EDC (albeit on a much smaller scale), PZ's projects are all separately funded. Each has its own agenda and expectations. School-based work at PZ is a collection of related endeavors rather than a systematically structured effort like SDP or CES. In part, the organization's work has acquired this characteristic as a result of the push and pull of various funders, each of whom has firm ideas about the "right" direction for a particular project. These multiple "right" directions have not allowed for the conscious development of an explicit theory of action with respect to school reform. Nevertheless, something of the sort has developed anyway, as we learned in our interviews. It takes the form of a theory in use that we sketch below, one that has been influenced by the principles we sketched above, and spread across PZ by means of its strong organizational culture.

STARTING WHERE TEACHERS ARE

At Project Zero, the phrase, "You've got to start where teachers are," is likely to be followed by an admonitory tale like the one Tom Hatch told us. He managed the After School Project, a partnership between PZ and a Boston elementary school. The purpose of this project, from the PZ perspective, was to design project-based curriculum incorporating recent ideas in assessment, collaborative learning, and the teaching of thinking. The goal was to contribute to within-school teaching and learning. However, the researchers chose an after-school context because they regarded it as likely to be a more fruitful one for research and development, less encumbered with constraining structures and expectations. The principal and teachers who agreed to become involved knew the researchers' goal, but they had a goal of their own: They wanted to have a good after-school program.

"We thought that they already had an established after-school program," Hatch explained, "but they thought we were going to help them design the program from scratch and get it up and running." The researchers were surprised to find "no schedule, no team, no system of getting snacks or supplies, no supervision, no rules, none of these basic things." In such circumstances, necessity would seem to dictate the first move, but, as Hatch explained, it is not always easy for researchers to put their agenda on hold. "During our first meetings, we would ask our partners, 'How can we help you?' We wanted them to say things like, 'I'm having a problem getting kids to write better,' so that we could help them with curriculum. But we would ask this question and the teacher would say, 'I need six hats for a drama production, or magic markers for an art project.' I just kept saying, 'We can't really provide that for you, but don't you want some help with your curriculum?' Finally, however, around Christmas time, we realized that *yes*, they did need six hats and if we ever wanted to get to the curriculum, we had to make sure that those practical needs—basic needs—were met first."

In discussing first steps in partnerships, PZ staff also spoke to us often about the importance of clarifying goals and establishing a shared agenda. In the After School Project, while the principal, teachers, and researchers agreed to focus on projects, each had somewhat different ideas of the purpose of the focus—even within the context of the after-school program, and quite apart from any curriculum aim. The PZ team wanted to support the development of students' literacy and thinking skills. The principal shared these concerns, but wanted more to help students do better on standardized tests. Meanwhile, the teachers wanted their students to experience success in activities that were not part of the regular school day, on the theory that this success might spill over. Finally, the students just wanted a safe, fun place to go after school. According to Hatch, the partners spent much of the first year sitting down together, trying to understand each other's different expectations, and figuring out how to accommodate them all.

Other PZ staff members have learned that listening closely to their partners early on in the process may make or break a new collaboration. The APPLE project researchers learned through several collaborations to be as explicit as possible about who they were and what they wanted to do. Just as important, however, they learned to subordinate their own interests to the agenda of the partner school. To listen closely, and put a partner's agenda first, lends momentum that eventually benefits the research. Another PZ researcher found that simply allowing a partner teacher to express herself—to say whatever was on her mind regardless of its connection to the research agenda—was the key to building a partnership that had until then been frustrating and unproductive. "I spent the time, made the time, stole it from something else. I can hardly think of anything more valuable that I experienced in a whole week of interviews. Yet, all it was, was that somebody heard her agenda."

Beginning a partnership well, in the view of some PZ staff, also means figuring out what ideas and strengths Project Zero can best provide in a given circumstance and basing this on the best possible assessment of the circumstance. The range of PZ's experience allows its researchers to find different starting points for partnerships with different teachers. "I think," said Mara Krechevsky, "that we try to help people wherever they're starting, help them identify needs, strengths, see what resources or expertise we can bring to bear after they've identified goals." Krechevsky suggested that this sort of facilitation may be what PZ is best suited for in the work of school reform—helping teachers assess where they are and suggesting appropriate ways to move forward. Tina Blythe agreed with Krechevsky's appraisal. A good example, she claimed, is the Teaching for Understanding Project, which "provides a framework or a way for teachers to get clear about what it is they're trying to have students understand in class, a framework that doesn't have any particular agenda to pursue, except helping kids learn deeply."

SHARING EXPERTISE

Tom Hatch told us that starting points are inconsequential in and of themselves—that what matters is where they lead and how much learning is generated along the way. "You can start with portfolios. If you use portfolios you might find ideas to improve your curriculum. That might lead you to projects. Then you'll start doing projects, but you'll find that kids aren't understanding as well as you had hoped. They're having fun, they're getting engaged, they're doing more work, but they're not getting the deep learning that you'd like. So that leads you to teaching for understanding."

But what is the thread that connects these learning moves? According to many of our PZ interviewees, it is a relationship in which both partners are viewed as contributing valuable expertise. The cachet of being an academic researcher—and a researcher working at Harvard and with Howard Gardner—provides entry into numerous schools and classrooms. But it also leads some teachers to view PZ researchers as "the experts," to request instructions on how to "do MI" or how to "do portfolios." Yet, as Noel White commented, Project Zero researchers at the same time may be looking to *teachers* as the experts, and at the opportunity to collaborate with them as an opportunity for their own learning. The combination sometimes has produced a kind of stalemate.

Steve Seidel told us the story of how one such stalemate broke. Two years into their collaboration with a small elementary school in rural Massachusetts, Seidel and his colleagues on the APPLE project joined the school's faculty in a periodic "roundtable" discussion of how things were going in the school's experiments with portfolios. As the group discussed problems in the work, tension grew. None of the teachers seemed to have ready solutions for the problems that surfaced in the discussion, and the PZ researchers were silent. This had happened before, and the researchers were silent as before because they felt no less stumped than the teachers. However, the teachers did not know that this was the reason for the silence. "Even after 2 years of close work with us," Seidel told us, "they held onto the notion that we had all the answers to their questions but were unwilling, for some reason, to share them." As the tension mounted this day, one of the teachers finally looked at the researchers, and—partly exasperated, partly relieved—blurted out, "Oh, wait. I get it! You guys really *don't* have the answers!"

Deference toward researchers is not the only obstacle PZ staff members have experienced in trying to build relationships with teachers. The relative youth of many PZ researchers and the inexperience of many in school settings may cause teachers to doubt the value of a partnership. Moreover, even for the most experienced members of the PZ staff, the Harvard name can be a stigma. In one instance, Seidel—a veteran high school teacher in Boston and Cambridge—and his PZ colleague Joe Walters—a former math teacher—arrived at La Guardia Airport on their way to work at a New York City school. When they emerged from the gate area, they found the driver sent to meet them holding a sign that read, "Two guys from Harvard." "Needless to say," Walters told us, "this was not the start of a particularly productive relationship."

Issues of expertise—who has it and who doesn't—are common in all school reformers' experience. They are especially inherent, however, in the dynamic between practitioners and researchers, inasmuch as researchers often are perceived by teachers to have more power, resources, and prestige than the teachers. The fact that the researchers actually may lack all these things goes unnoticed. In the PZ view, researchers do have certain discrete expertise, as do teachers. In practice, however, PZ researcher Julie Viens told us, a good move is to play down discrete expertise and play up "co-expertise." After trying various approaches with school-based partners, she found success when she emphasized that she and her school colleagues would be "co-experts, co-learners, and co-researchers."

In the face of the expertise dilemma, the researchers involved in the APPLE project tried something quite different. They asked partner teachers to join them in an exploration of student work, one that focused on particular pieces of work and avoided making judgments about them. Although this is an activity that by its nature calls upon diverse expertise, and may be a new experience for both researchers and teachers alike, it is also one that privileges the researcher's ways of looking. The project asked the teachers to take on a new role, and a difficult one: observing without judging, looking closely at detail, considering all aspects of a work, thinking about it in its uniqueness rather than in comparison to other works. In effect, the APPLE researchers deliberately surfaced the expertise dilemma and resolved to work through it. As Joe Walters told us, this was because the activity they planned got immediately to the heart of APPLE's approach: "Students' work is at the center. The approach is not theoretical. There's not a lot of talk about child development, constructivist learning. It's basically, 'Here's what a kid did—let's talk about it.'"

But whether by dealing directly with some gap in expertise, or by finding areas of co-expertise, building relationships between researchers and
teachers takes patience and time. Most PZ researchers have had the patience, although few have had enough time. Tied to research agendas and
funding schedules, the collaborations are in most cases only 3 or 4 years
long. With few exceptions, therefore, PZ has not enjoyed the "space" in
its relationships with schools that CES or SDP gains by basing such relationships on long-term membership status. As a result, although PZ has
developed moves to help teachers begin to work with new ideas, it has
little understanding of how these teachers fare once the partnership ends.
Growing dissatisfaction with its ordinarily temporary alliances has
prompted PZ to consider how it might develop partnerships that have a
good chance of enduring beyond first steps and next steps. This, among
other reasons, drew it to the ATLAS partnership.

SUPPORTING SCHOOLWIDE CHANGE

Over the years, Project Zero has watched many of its partner teachers
struggle to sustain their work in schools where colleagues, administrators,
and even parents express indifference or opposition. We heard one story
of a teacher collaborating on a PZ project who was visited by members of
a district evaluation team. Skeptical about the methods they saw in his
classroom—involving students up and out of their chairs, working on their
own or talking together—the evaluators told the teacher that they'd come
back "when there was real teaching going on."

As the result of such experiences, PZ has decided that isolated experimentation in the classroom is tenuous at best; that supportive environments are critical. Unlike CES and SDP, however, PZ has not developed a
coherent "schoolwide" approach to sustainable school change. There are
no "Project Zero schools" or systematic PZ approaches to organizational
change, no Common Principles, no Gardner Process. On the other hand,
while PZ has not changed its basic strategy of forming partnerships with
teachers in classrooms, it recently has sought to ensure that these partnerships thrive in their contexts and beyond the limited time frames of
the partnership.

The most straightforward of its moves in this direction has involved
finding partner teachers who *already* work in supportive schools. While
most PZ projects have no set policies regarding which schools to work with
or not work with, staff members have developed some ideas of what to
look for. These are things like safety from excessive criticism, tolerance
for experimentation and taking risks, flexibility for teachers to build on

their own strengths, supportive leadership, and regularly scheduled blocks of time for teachers to talk to one another and to share innovative practices. And many PZ staff we talked to said they look for schools that are "reflective."

It's important to say that Project Zero has worked with many schools that do *not* meet these criteria. But the emergence of the criteria suggests the emergence of a PZ identity as school reformer. In one recent project, PZ got to exercise this new identity in ways that suggest SDP or CES. In the MassNet project, a collaboration between PZ and the Massachusetts Department of Education, PZ researchers had the opportunity to pick the schools they would work with from a large pool of applicants. The PZ team picked partners that exhibited what Joe Walters referred to as an "absence of barriers." As an absolute prerequisite, each school had to demonstrate that its potential participation had the support of at least 75% of its faculty, as well as the explicit support of the principal and district administration. Once they had narrowed the initial pool of 50 applicant schools to 17, the MassNet researchers conducted visits to each school to select a final five. As Walters recounted, they looked for "signs that the faculty had taken on any kind of schoolwide initiatives—that they had worked as a group on anything, the presence of schoolwide decision-making bodies, evidence of project-based curriculum and more authentic kinds of assessment. But none of this was a necessity. We weren't looking for people who had already done it, but a readiness to do." In addition to assessing the schools' readiness relative to specific criteria, the team also spent time observing less formally. By roaming the hallways, engaging students and teachers in informal conversation—finding out whether doors were open, whether interaction was frequent, constructive and friendly, etc.—the researchers were able to gain a clear sense of each school in action. These observations helped them to pick schools that they felt would be capably committed to the partnership. Of course, like both SDP and CES, they later found great variance in this commitment.

Besides merely finding presumably supportive schools, PZ also has recently explored helping to make schools more supportive. The APPLE Project, for example, has experimented with a move that it calls "opening the doors." APPLE found that indifference or hostility toward classroom experimentation may occur simply because a community has not had the chance to witness or understand the new work, particularly in controversial areas like assessment. Because experimentation seems risky, teachers and researchers in a research and development partnership may tend instinctually to conceal their work from parents and even other teachers, to "keep the doors closed." This, of course, exacerbates distrust. In one instance, a group of parents at a partner elementary school waged a public campaign to protest their children's participation in the APPLE work. The researchers realized in retrospect that they had been partly responsible for the public outcry. At the start of the project they had made little effort to tell parents who they were, what they were doing at the school, and why they thought the new work was a worthwhile endeavor. As Steve Seidel later concluded, this instinct to "protect" the work was counterproductive—the researchers instead should have invited parents in to see the work—in parent–teacher meetings, open houses, and exhibitions of student work. Opening the doors to the community in this way may not ensure support, Seidel noted, but keeping the doors closed "assures no support."

A third move that Project Zero has employed to ensure supportive environments for the teachers it works with is to build relationships with reform organizations that have schoolwide school reform expertise. ATLAS itself is probably the best example of this approach. In ATLAS, PZ sought to complement its classroom-level expertise with the schoolwide expertise of SDP and CES. In addition to ATLAS, PZ has worked closely with the Massachusetts Department of Education and with the Alliance Schools, a growing reform network in Texas, among others.

A final move that the organization has made to build supportive environments for teachers has been to develop methods and resources that encourage teachers to develop relationships with other teachers—both within their own schools and outside them. Like the national faculty initiatives developed at CES, PZ's Regional Assessment Network (RAN) allows teachers in the Massachusetts area to come together once a month to discuss their PZ-related assessment experimentation. RAN's meetings are implicitly designed to support a cross-school community of teachers to supplement within-school communities.

Project Zero's efforts to ensure that classroom practice is supported by the broader environment are forcing the organization to become more systemic in its approach to school reform. The Massachusetts Schools Network, the ATLAS partnership, and similar collaborations are pulling it into new territory and demanding that it gain new expertise. How the organization responds to the demand will determine in large part what it looks like in its next decade.

GENERATING AND PUSHING BIG IDEAS

For the moment, however, PZ as school reformer remains distinctly different from SDP and CES. For these organizations, the goal is changing schools—lots of them—and ideas are a tool. For PZ, ideas are the goal, and the direct impact of the ideas in changing schools is still secondary. When we asked Howard Gardner to contrast PZ with its ATLAS partners, he told us that PZ is primarily an "idea-generating place," a place that was, in fact, born of a set of ideas. Nelson Goodman was a philosopher, and his influence on the approach of the young Project Zero was profound. As Gardner told us, "Philosophers' work stops when they've clarified a question. Occasionally they might think about the answer. Goodman used to say that a psychologist was just a philosopher with a research grant."

Project Zero, Gardner claimed, has come a long way in following up on its ideas, but the ideas themselves still take center stage. He spoke of how some staff come to PZ expecting to do "school reform," but soon become frustrated by the amount of time and energy devoted to thinking, clarifying, and conceptualizing. From Gardner's point of view, to be successful at PZ, you've got to be able to find enjoyment in the conceptual work alone. The other ATLAS partners, in his view, reverse the emphasis.

Gardner added, however, that PZ has always tried to give its ideas "a push in the right direction." Yet it has never developed a coherent approach toward how to do this, or given it the prominence it may deserve. In fact, for many PZ staff and projects, writing articles and producing other products happens after the "real" work has been done. Until recently, staff was expected to do much of that "follow-up" work after hours, and, in some cases, after the research grant had been used up. Similarly, requests for workshops and presentations typically have been handled on a case-by-case basis and ultimately filled by staff members who can manage to find some extra time.

But this reticence at PZ concerning dissemination may no longer be feasible, according to Gardner. The demand for what it has been learning is relentless: from educators who need support; from markets that want articles, products, presentations, and workshops; from funders that want impact; and from the pressures of knowing that if PZ won't build on its own work, then other organizations will, often distorting it in the process. Julie Viens talked to us about the challenge of developing a response to all this demand: "We began to provide professional development out of necessity, the people in the field wanting our help. We want to be flexible about what it is that we can offer. At the same time, I think we need to come up with some bottom-line standards for approaching professional development because I think we're just such a mixed bag."

The creation of the PZ Summer Institute was among the first steps in developing a systematic approach to dissemination. At the first Institute, held in 1996, 100 participants, mostly teachers and administrators from the United States and overseas, attended a week-long series of workshops in which PZ staff introduced the work of the organization—a kind of mini-

Fall Forum. Like the latter, the Institute eschewed didactic formats and in a sense enacted PZ by having attendees work on projects. More than 30 PZ staff and related practitioners worked closely with the participants throughout the sessions.

In addition, PZ recently has created several staff positions to assume explicit responsibilities for dealing with dissemination and products. Shirley Veenema, a veteran PZ staff member and visual artist, has taken a leadership role in this effort and hopes to help PZ expand the audience for its work. One example of her effort is that the 1997 Summer Institute, called the MIND Symposium, was constructed not only as an actual event in Boston but also as a virtual event on the World Wide Web. As part of a bigger, long-term project, Veenema and a small team of colleagues are developing a Project Zero Internet service that will allow subscribers to have regular access to PZ publications, discussion groups, and so on.

Veenema sees her role as gauging Project Zero's potential for reaching broad audiences and helping the organization design a strategic approach. Frustrated by PZ's historical inattention to dissemination, she sees a current window of opportunity to address the problem. Veenema agrees with Howard Gardner's observation that demand for PZ work has grown so much that responding to it on a case-by-case basis is no longer tenable. PZ will have to move beyond its habitual practice of wrapping up a project with research articles, she told us. She also talked about the growing need for the organization to generate revenue from its projects. Research grants no longer will fully sustain the work, she said. The organization must get serious about "going to market" and must adopt entrepreneurial approaches to doing work that makes money. She finds it ironic, she added, that the home of MI theory presents most of its work in a limited, print-based format.

Several staff at PZ agreed with Veenema's approach, but suggested that it will require fundamental changes in the way the organization structures its tasks and its time. More time must be devoted exclusively to dissemination, products, and outreach in general. For example, the first PZ Summer Institute, while successful in meeting its educational goals, exhausted those staff members who contributed to its production, pulling them away from their usual work without additional support. Projects must consider dissemination and products as an integral aspect of the work from the outset. And project funders must be convinced of the value of such an approach.

But as considerable energy focuses on these new directions, the "outreach" initiatives tend to come into conflict with the original mission and the basic principles of the organization. In our conversations at PZ, we found both optimism about the possibilities of dissemination and concerns that such dissemination may not support the kind of deep learning that has long been the focus of PZ's work. According to Tina Blythe, having more materials and resources available may make it less necessary for PZ researchers to provide on-site assistance to those wishing to implement change, but this will mean in turn a loss of learning opportunities for the PZ researchers. "It's still very unclear what should be," she said.

On the other hand, there is the tension between the traditional mission of PZ as a research organization—whether learning on site or off—and the demands of its emerging identity as school reformer. Even with his enthusiasm for PZ's new directions, Gardner remains convinced that as school reformer, PZ's greatest potential lies in its capacity to keep generating ideas. "As the idea makers fade away," he said, referring perhaps to his own role, "it's important to get new idea makers."

CHAPTER 5

Snapshots of Education Development Center

Several years ago, Jan Hawkins moved the entire Center for Children and Technology, an already functioning group of research-based reformers, from Bank Street College into EDC. Naturally, Hawkins and her colleagues had to size up the culture of their new home. One of the conclusions they reached early is that EDC's work is almost always about "changing people's minds." There are lots of other ways to make moves on the educational status quo, Hawkins told us, but EDC seems to think first about changing minds. Of course, there are also lots of ways of working to change people's minds, and EDC has tried many of them—including ambitious national efforts to redirect curriculum. But when an organization sees its business as changing people's minds, it cannot afford to work wholly at a big scale. How else can it know whether its efforts are succeeding than by close-ups of particular clients' practice? This is why the biggest of the ATLAS partner organizations—with more capital, more employees, more scope, and, arguably, more ambition than the other three combined—also practices its change efforts in as intimate a way as they do. It is also why EDC avoids choosing between large-scale systemic interventions and small-scale ones. It is an attitude that has been honed by its long and complex history as a change-oriented organization.

BIG AMBITIONS

The organization now known as EDC began in 1958 as Educational Services Incorporated (ESI), an entity designed to administer the continuing development of PSSC Physics, the first federally funded curriculum project. This was the year that President Eisenhower signed into law the National Defense Education Act, preparing the way for an unparalleled investment of federal dollars in elementary and secondary curriculum, and ensuring that PSSC Physics would have progeny. The course took its name from the Physical Science Study Committee at MIT, which de-

veloped it. And ESI took much of its culture from MIT's postwar ebul-
lience. As Peter Dow (1991) puts it, ESI "attacked the curriculum challenge with the confidence of those who had mastered radar and the atom
bomb" (p. 28). And it matched the confidence with the method. It
planned to convene other "study committees" to create other curricula
that, it presumed, would transform American education as other technologies were beginning in those days to transform many aspects of
American life.

Within a few years, however, the young organization had managed
to acquire a sense of the differences between education, and, say, the
aviation industry. It recognized that innovations in curriculum cannot
by themselves transform an enterprise so dependent on cellular interactions between a single teacher and some children. Transformation in
such a field must depend as well on a host of interrelated innovations of
structure and culture and expertise that demand, in turn, deep learning
and unlearning among many people playing many roles. Ellen Wahl
(1995), an anthropologist who is studying EDC, describes the immedi-
ate consequences for the organization of this emerging sense of the systemic nature of its target.

> As EDC grew, curriculum development by itself was recognized as too con-
> fined and EDC expanded its work to encompass the organizations, systems,
> and communities in which learning takes place. In 1967, the leadership of
> Educational Services Incorporated merged ESI with the Institute for Educa-
> tional Innovation to become EDC. The new organization combined the pow-
> erful curriculum reform projects of PSSC Physics, Elementary Science Study,
> and the African Education Program with grounded change efforts in pilot
> communities that were trying to effect reform. (p. 4)

The Institute for Educational Innovation was the first regional education
lab for New England, launched by the pioneering Elementary and Secondary Education Act of 1965. Thus the new partnership was a marriage
of federal initiatives, one aimed at the development of national curricula,
the other at strengthening local capacity for reform. It was a very rocky
marriage at first, according to Ed Campbell (1974), with each partner stub-
bornly resisting the integration of perspectives.

> Some members of ESI believed that the principal way to bring about educa-
> tional change was through new curricular materials, whereas some mem-
> bers of IEI believed that the principal way to achieve reform was by working
> directly in school systems to change teacher attitudes, organizational rela-
> tionships, and school–community relationships. (p. 15)

Yet, partly as a result of the coaxing Campbell provided in his EDC presidency and later the explicit direction provided by Janet Whitla in hers, the marriage of design and service has survived. Although EDC today is long out of the business of running a regional lab, it has managed since those days to keep its design work highly grounded in actual places and to acquire a major reputation as a site-based catalyst of reform. Barbara Scott Nelson explained for us the connection between the impulse to design for reform and the impulse to activate it in particular places.

> I think people at EDC are not content to make a widget and put it out there, and when I say *widget*, I don't just mean physical things, but ideas too. By and large, people at EDC want to understand what it would mean for people to have that widget in their worlds and how the widget would actually help them go forward with something. And how do you have to design the widget, not so that it is comfortable to use, but so that it makes growing and changing possible.

In this chapter, we look at EDC's theory of action by means of snapshots of the practices of particular EDC staff members. We have taken these snapshots from different points along a strategic continuum that runs from small-scale activism in school reform to large-scale activism. We try to see the strategies through the moves, and the overall theory of action from the ground up. Thus we try to mimic the overall paradox that marks EDC as a whole: a massive organization with an intimate style. In the process, we depart from the style of the previous three chapters that each began with a presentation of principles or espoused theory. Here, we save that for last. The reason has to do with EDC's massiveness, and with the fact that in marked contrast to its ATLAS partners, it is not a single-purpose organization. It also has to do with the subtle ways in which the EDC mission tends to be expressed within the organization. In other words, espoused theory tends to be espoused more quietly at EDC than at the other ATLAS organizations. Indeed, our interviewees at EDC nearly all expressed skepticism at some point during their interviews that we actually could see anything of the whole of the EDC theory of action in the limited parts we were exploring.

We are pleased to report, however, that in reading the results, they all agreed that we had gotten at least that part of the whole that we intended to capture. This is the part that deals with school reform. Yet, we acknowledge that there are other sides of EDC than the one that fosters school reform, many other strategies than the ones we examine, and countless other moves.

INTIMATE INTERVENTIONS

EDC staff member Cathy Morocco believes that prospects for serious school reform depend especially on teachers' images of learning. To have schools that promote powerful learning, teachers must draw continuously on their own sense of what powerful learning looks like and sounds like. Luckily, she told us, everyone has experienced deep learning at one time or another and carries a latent image of it. Still, "unless we tap into that or create new experiences that build on that prior knowledge, people will not necessarily get it." Therefore, in her view, systemic school reform is only as good as its capacity to reach deeply into teachers' minds.

Morocco's theory of action has personal as well as theoretical roots. In this respect, she is like nearly everyone else interviewed across the four organizations we studied. To illustrate how she works, for example, she told us the story of an interaction she had with her own son's teacher, one that started out as a parent–teacher conference. From Morocco's point of view, the conference was about a son losing ground in math for want of any breathing space in a frantic curriculum. From the teacher's point of view, it was about a student who needed to work harder to catch up. Moments into the conference, however, it became something else for both of them. Morocco sensed that the teacher was "caught up in the mill" of textbook coverage and SAT preparation, "but knew some other reality very deeply." Morocco likes to ferret out such deeper "reality" whenever she senses it and to encourage reflection on it. In this case, she discovered that the teacher had gone to school in another country, "where they do not have tests that have 25 or 30 problems done in a short time period, but four or five challenging problems and students have all the time that they need in order to do them." Putting aside for a moment her interests as a mother, Morocco huddled with this teacher around this recollected image of learning. They tried collaboratively to make it an occasion for the teacher's professional growth.

Such huddling is what Morocco has long done in teacher inquiry groups focused on the teaching of writing, language arts, science, or other subjects, or in conversations with teachers based on transcribed interactions between them and specific children. It is a common move at EDC and is especially interesting for what seems its rejection of the argument that working for change one teacher at a time is futile. But the huddling has a bigger purpose than is obvious. We may not discern it because, as Morocco told us, "normally, the micro and the macro come unhinged in school reform." We are used to the fact that efforts to change larger contexts somehow lose touch with how people really think about teaching and learning, and overlook the need to affect this thinking. The point of the huddling, as Morocco and her EDC colleagues practice it, is not merely to affect one teacher's practice—although that is one objective—but to have the power to affect many others' practice by virtue of being continually intimate with what changing practice entails. Then, of course, they seek to bring what they learn in the micro out into the macro, to hinge the local to the global. So, Morocco, for example, is currently working on a project in Long Beach, California, where she has designed small study groups focused on explorations of the district's curriculum standards. In this work, she told us, "intimacy and teacher change are in the foreground, but the work connects with and helps to drive systemic change around a larger district mission—namely, achieving higher standards for every student in a culturally diverse and largely poor community."

Of course, her Long Beach huddling differs from the other example offered above in that it was invited. "The most powerful collaborations come from outsiders being invited into schools," Morocco has written with Project Zero's Mara Krechevsky (Krechevsky & Morocco, 1996), although the "outsiders often need to lay the groundwork for creating informed invitations"(p. 3). The best invitations, in Morocco's view, are based on a "graspable image" of authentic learning and teaching. Otherwise, the partners may lack a shared sense of what's worth working on and of where the work is headed, making the intervention seem an intrusion.

What's a "graspable image?" Morocco offered the example of the expeditions that form the metaphoric basis of a school design project inspired by Outward Bound and—like ATLAS—launched by the New American Schools Development Corporation (NASDC).

> Expeditionary Learning takes people out and says, "Forget school. You are too locked into that. Go out, and let's do a canoeing trip where you have to support each other, where you don't know what the next task is, where you are testing some new skills. Get back in touch with what it means to really explore something, and then you can come back to school and realize that what you are ordinarily doing is driving your kids through experiences that are too set."[1]

By contrast, ATLAS, according to Morocco, had initial difficulty generating a graspable image of a "community for authentic teaching and learning." It seemed to her that its signature term, *pathway,* suggested only "structural and organizational" continuity among the different levels of a school system and was no more evocative of authentic teaching and learning than, say, "vertical curricular articulation." Then, "at one of the first meetings of the ATLAS community," she told us, "I sat with Debbie Meier, and the way she talked about the pathway, I got it and I've never lost it." What was different was that Meier spoke of the *child's* pathway and imagined it as a uniquely coherent and community-generated approach to a particular child's learning, rather than a prescribed route for all children.

We refer to Morocco's work as having a personal quality. However, a characteristic of most of the moves we uncovered in all our interviews across all the ATLAS partners was their curiously dual status as personal and organizational expression. In several respects, for example, Morocco's huddling and her reliance on graspable images are as deeply EDC as they are deeply Morocco. For one thing, both tactics seem founded on question posing. How did you yourself learn math? How does an expedition contrast with school as it ordinarily is? Janet Whitla (1996), long-term president of EDC, has written that question posing is "at the heart of EDC's work . . . that the best of EDC's projects over the decades have engaged people, young and old, in raising and finding answers to questions of importance in their lives" (p. 7).

Morocco's work also reflects another long-established EDC habit. This is the focus on understanding as it manifests itself within particular subjects of the school curriculum. EDC began with an effort to reinvent the teaching of high school physics. Today, although it undertakes projects on many other facets of education, its school-oriented projects still tend to be rooted in the perspectives of particular subjects. Although this focus is partly the consequence of funding streams, it is intentional too. EDC staff member Molly Watt told us, "EDC has a very strong philosophy that professional development has to be about something." Brian Lord, another veteran EDC staff member, suggested that this *something* is frequently the subjects that teachers teach, because these anchor policy aspirations. To bring the latter "to scale," he said, reformers must begin their work "closer to home." Implicit in his view—and the view seems pervasive at EDC—is the idea that one can come no closer to the core of teaching than to affect a teacher's sense of what to teach. Change a teacher's mind about that, the implicit theory goes, and much else will shift in the teacher's practice, as well as in the systems that enmesh it.

Finally, Morocco's work is pure EDC insofar as it involves, in EDC staff member Barbara Scott Nelson's word, "dis-equilibration." That is, Morocco's moves as a reformer are always intended to dislodge some system—whether that of a particular teacher's testing practices, or of a particular school's habit of teaching writing or using technology—from its current state into a more desirable one. "In order to play that role," as Nelson admitted to us, "you have to have an image of where you think that system could be." EDC is never the neutral facilitator, and in this respect, is quite like its three ATLAS partners.

LEARNING COMMUNITIES

Like Cathy Morocco's, Molly Watt's work as an EDC reform agent is tied into her own experience and intuition. Director of EDC's Action Research Center, Watt told us with a laugh, that "as a child, I was a child-researcher." Throughout her career, she continued, she has been involved in educational change efforts "and part of being involved in these changes had to do with being part of a group of colleagues that in some way or other were studying the change, gathering evidence about the change, trying to determine how we knew if anything was happening, seeing how we could communicate that to parents or other teachers or whoever the heck our audience was." She originally left classroom teaching, she said, because she got too many glimpses of the way that the larger system impinges on classrooms, and she wanted to do something about it. "I figured all these good ideas were nothing if there was no one to sign the requisition for, sand." In her experience, administrators were always more ready to buy basal readers than sand. So, she became an administrator herself, and later—seeking to affect a still larger share of the impinging context, a consultant. Ultimately, this career trajectory led to EDC. As consultant, she has specialized in the educational uses of computing, but this has been, she told us, merely her "Trojan horse. If you have some object that people deem important, you can gather a group of them around it in a learning community."

The convening of learning communities is a widespread EDC practice. Watt explained the strategy as follows:

> In order to change, you need to take time out of the dailiness of life. You need to take on a learning stance, or what I call a research frame of mind. When taking a look, you can be just as interested in something that's working, something that's not working, being curious as to why, wondering what would happen if, seeing what more you can find out about it—these are what I mean by "research frame of mind." It is different from the frame of mind that most of us take on as practitioners: We're asserting louder, heavier, stronger; we're not necessarily taking a look. So, this is a way to take a look.

How does Watt help people acquire such a frame of mind? She told us that she tries to help them construct "their island out of time" in as mundane a context as possible, close to work, among their closest colleagues. The point is to routinize the process of inquiry, to make it possible for people to engage in it "regularly over time, over a year, over

2 years, over 3 years, over 4 years, with a group of people that you can really become honest with." To get the process started, Watt tries to stir up something among them.

> They think I am going to give them a pleasant little day of lectures or videotapes, but that's not what I do. What I do is I go and try to stir up some fervor about questions they have and discrepancies they see in their own work. I use these as a way to set up how they could go about studying them.

"It's not like a formula," she said, yet there are specifiable components to this move. One is the stimulation of a general curiosity that is nonetheless full of quirky difference. The difference becomes something to discuss, and the discussion is crucial. Crucial too is the habit of searching for evidence and identifying both the resources already available and the ones that must be sought. "Frequently," she explained, "people in these groups will say, 'I realized I don't know anything about how to conduct on-line searches,' or 'I don't really know how to discuss methodology,' or 'I don't really understand what the kids are learning when they roll balls down the ramp that are different weights.'" Watt seeks to move them past such important admissions toward asking, as she put it, "Is there someone in this group here, or should we invite someone in to help us learn these things?" She also clearly engages in the move that Barbara Scott Nelson calls "going meta." That is, Watt manages to get the people working in her learning communities to consider why this way of learning is productive and how it may be so for children as well as adults.

> The ways I work are all very similar to the way I believe we're asking teachers to change in their educational approaches with kids. I don't mean they're a one-to-one comparison, but we're asking teachers to support kids in being more like scientists, mathematicians, writers. So I try to work, wherever I start, with establishing a similar kind of learning community. I don't necessarily make that an evident statement. I make sure it comes out in the reflections when we look back, but I don't really have to make sure. It always comes out. Someone always says it, and I can count on that. But if someone didn't say it, I would.

Obviously, a crucial component of these moves is Watt herself. Although the point is to enable people to carry on by themselves in these learning communities, and even to teach others to do so within adjacent parts of the system, still, Watt told us, someone has to "bring the vision in." Among the

ATLAS partners, as we discovered in our research, there is considerable variation in the comfort level associated with *bringing the vision in*. Of course, all four organizations do it, but EDC is perhaps the most explicit in accounting for how this may be done and why it is critical.

The impulse goes way back in the organization's history. Jerrold Zacharias, the MIT physicist who generally is acknowledged as the founder of EDC, saw the entrenched localism of his era as a chief source of anti-intellectualism in American education (Wahl, 1995b). He regarded the smart outside reformer as a counterweight to parochialism. In today's EDC, many find the physical metaphor unappealing, preferring a more organic one. Barbara Scott Nelson recalled for us Eleanor Duckworth's distinction between the ways the physicists involved in EDC's seminal project, the Elementary Science Study, talked about Piaget, and the way the biologists did (Duckworth, 1987, p. 34). In EDC's 1991 Annual Report, referring to the respective roles in educational change of the local and the global, Janet Whitla eschewed science metaphors altogether. She used the musical term *counterpoint*, rather than *counterweight*: the combination of melodies rather than the opposition of forces. In either image, the outsider is crucial, but the shift of image matters too. Although Whitla, like Zacharias, regrets the localism in American education, which she thinks accounts for wasteful reinvention, she has a somewhat different idea of what EDC can do about it. EDC's role is not to bring the requisite broader knowledge to the locals, she told us, but rather "to link people first to other schools and universities in their own settings, and then to larger networks of teachers in other places, to help people tap into emerging practices so that they're not caught within their own limits."

EXPLORING VIRTUAL WORLDS

One way EDC practices raising people's sights is by means of case studies. EDC staff members Ilene Kantrov and Barbara Miller told us that cases have the power to function as "windows and mirrors." They give teachers and other educational practitioners access to other people's practices—a crucial developmental tool in a profession marked by localism. At the same time, this *other* practice can stimulate reflection on one's own—particularly when prompted by thoughtful facilitation. So, the 10 pages describing somebody else's dilemma or the 20-minute video capturing images from somebody else's classroom becomes, in effect, one's own virtual world of practice, a place to work out an understanding that may prove portable.

The way this works is counterintuitive, according to Miller. Initially, case discussion participants press the facilitators for more background on the case. What did the teacher do just before the scene we're watching? Who is the child in the red cap and why isn't he speaking? But Kantrov and Miller turn these questions back on the ones who ask them. Why do you want to know? Why is the question you're asking so important? They do so because they regard cases not as puzzles to be solved but as spurs to inquiry and to the discovery of multiple perspectives on reality. The tendency we all have, Miller claimed, "when we're wearing our problem-solving hats, is to whirl this problem down to the one most useful perspective." But there seldom is one. Referring to a case called "Oliver's Experiment," Kantrov asked rhetorically what the purpose would be of solving Oliver's dilemma in some definitive way. Instead, she said, "we can really value the perspectives that we all bring, and see that there are a variety of options that Oliver can take up depending on a lot of things." It is much better, she said, for people to walk away from Oliver's dilemma with a feeling that their own dilemmas, like his, might be open to various interpretations.

"What we really are trying to do," Kantrov said, "is push people away from the case rather than into the case." It turns out, she added, that people see very different things when they look into the window of somebody else's practical dilemma, "and then what becomes really interesting is to find out what they see and to reflect on why they see it." The point is to turn the window—carefully, thoughtfully, and respectfully—into a mirror. Thus cases—as Kantrov and Miller construe them—are neither exemplars for practice nor even instances of practice intended to illustrate abstract concepts or principles. In this respect, they contradict an assumption common in some school change efforts about the relation between theory and practice. "When cases are constructed as concrete examples of something you're trying to get across," Kantrov explained, "it's easy for people to say 'But it's not my concrete example, so it doesn't work for me.'" If there's an infinite number of cases to write, she told us, then it's because there are an infinite number of issues to deal with, not because there are an infinite number of contexts to be captured. The point is to enable people to enter a somewhat unfamiliar context, and within this context to find material they can use to construct their own portable understanding.

Sometimes it is only within an unfamiliar context that one can reach an understanding, particularly when complex and emotionally charged matters are involved. Janet Whitla told us that at EDC, "we often use case studies to get people to address particular topics that can be too hot to just discuss." Kantrov and Miller illustrated this with observations from a case-based workshop series they designed, called *Faces of Equity*. They designed *Faces of Equity* for the Michigan Partnership for New Education, a state-wide school reform effort. It is built around the exploration of equity and of equity in curriculum as these issues manifest themselves in half-hour videos of three classrooms and interviews of teachers and students.

The first video portrays scenes from Judith Richards's third-fourth grade classroom in Cambridge, Massachusetts, as well as interviews of Richards and her students. In one scene, a small group of students works on a math problem. Four of the children are active participants in the problem solving, but two boys hang back. After several minutes, one of these boys—the one in the blue cap—offers his first tentative contribution and before long joins in fully. But the other boy—the one in the red cap—never seems to connect. In fact, during the course of the 8-minute video segment, he never speaks once.

Miller: When people process what they see in the video, we get some people who could not see anything else—would not attend to anything else—they were so distressed about this boy. Then we also get people who don't seem to have noticed the problem.

Kantrov: "What kid are you talking about?" they'll say.
"The one in the baseball cap," someone will answer.
"But there were two kids in baseball caps."
"No, there was only one."

Miller: Every time we do this case, you can count on getting these two extremes. And the people who were very upset, who could focus only on this child, start to ask questions. They need to know all these things about this kid. And that becomes the opportunity to say, "Tell us why. Tell us what sense you made of him, what assumptions you've made."

Kantrov: Ultimately, we tell them that he is Haitian Creole, has come to this country only recently, and speaks no English. But if you tell that to people up front, that stops you from having the conversation about why it matters so much to one person and why another didn't notice it. We find that the people who didn't seem to notice Jean—it's not like their minds are blank. They are focused on something else that others didn't pick up on.

Miller: So the case offers an opportunity to understand that we filter what we pay attention to, and that the filter comes from some place, and we need to get on the table where those places are.

Kantrov: And even when people learn that Jean speaks no English, there is a next wave of opportunity. Some say, "Oh, Okay." And then somebody else asks, "What do you mean—'Oh, Okay?'" And we can ask, "So, why are you bothered by that?" In any group, you can count on multiple forks in the road.

Kantrov and Miller came together to work on the *Faces of Equity* and other print and video case-based projects from different EDC streams of work. Kantrov, having once taught English literature and writing in college, has worked at EDC for years on curriculum, software, and professional development—as a developer, researcher, and manager. Miller was a middle school teacher who went on to get a Harvard doctorate in human development under Carol Gilligan. She came to EDC to work on a teacher networking project, the Urban Math Collaboratives, and has gone on to work with teachers and districts on other aspects of professional development. "The people most likely to succeed at EDC," Kantrov told us, "are the people who are first of all flexible and also have many skills and interests." What happens then is that streams of work intersect over time as people seek connections to other people based on common interests and on funding opportunities that arise. Kantrov explained to us how this happened to Miller and her, and in the process describes a pattern that in its repetition over many years, streams of work, and funding opportunities has lent EDC much of its strategic coherence and also honed its overall theory of action.

> I was brought into a conversation that Barbara and some others were having with the Los Angeles Education Partnership (LAEP) about what was going to be a much larger project, and what happened is that Barb and I and Brian Lord were negotiating with LAEP and we realized pretty quickly that they were not going to fund the larger project we wanted to do. So we decided, Well, how can we both serve their interests and advance what *we* are interested in doing. And Barb and I had been talking about case work and how to pursue case work, so we ended up proposing some case work to LA, and there we were.

SYSTEMIC INTERVENTION

At first glance, Judi Sandler's work seems all focused on curriculum development. Indeed, for nearly a decade, she has worked on the design of science curriculum at EDC. However, most of this work has entailed site-based activism too. She told us the story of how the two came together in her experience.

> We started out with the development of this curriculum, and in order to develop the curriculum, we had to be fairly knowledgeable about what schools were currently doing. We had to think about

the implementation issues of good science, so that the curriculum would be very usable by teachers. We started to work with seven school districts. These school districts saw participating in the development of a national curriculum as the ultimate professional development experience. Teachers were consultants to our project; they met on a regular basis and formed a core team in their communities. In one major city, this group was 14 elementary teachers who were fairly representative of the teachers in the district. None of them had any science background. The district saw that these people were meeting on a regular basis to talk about our curriculum, and, very smartly, the science supervisor said, "Well, maybe because they are the only people talking about science in our district, we'd like to share the agenda. We will use half of the agenda to work on supporting your curriculum, and the other half will be to get these people to start to think about what the city should be thinking about in terms of changing science."

In telling this story of co-opted design, Sandler pointed out that all she and her colleagues needed from this district were some teacher consultants. The designers need not have waded into deeper waters, yet they felt obligated by their expertise: "We had built this incredible knowledge base in developing our curriculum," and, in the process, "were forced to look at what was happening across the country." One cannot expect, she explained, that a single district will have any such breadth of perspective on either the problems of teaching better science or the possible solutions to these problems. "So, we have a lot of stuff that we feel we are in a position to share, not impose."

Moreover, there was an invitation in hand—always a powerful motivation at EDC. And it was not only the science supervisor's invitation, but the teachers' also: "This group started to think about a plan for restructuring, and called themselves the Restructuring Science Group." Sandler's small band of designer-activists could not resist.

We said, "Even if we cannot really support you, let's see if we can get some funding. We will apply to the Department of Education and the National Science Foundation. Somebody out there might want to support the district. We thought it would be interesting for other districts to see what this city was doing because they were looking at decentralization.

We were fortunate to get funding from both the Department of Education and from the National Science Foundation. We convinced the funders that this would be a wonderful experiment in cost sharing.

Then, with funding in place, Sandler and her colleagues played a critical backstage role in ensuring that the effort went somewhere.

> The 14 teachers in our group worked on and presented to their school board a reform plan about how we need to think differently about science in the community. While we were very involved in helping them think about the science and using that as a lever, we essentially created a model for change for them which was to build leadership at the site level using teacher leaders, as well as district-wide support from resource specialists and lots of support in training. A lot of emphasis was placed on an action team at the school site—namely, these teacher leaders working with principals and other teachers.
>
> This was the first large-scale project like that in this city, but they now have a new math project that was just funded, which the district instituted. What they are trying to do now is build the same kind of expertise in math, join leaders at the school site, following the same model that we used in science. Meanwhile, a new super-intendent came in, and her approach is to create a whole reform structure for the district—to establish district goals in every subject area, but in the context of community-based schools and their different identities—that's her platform. So, the science piece fits very nicely, and they are using the school-site leadership model that we instituted with them, as sort of a universal way to think about change.

Lately, Sandler's role as "technical assister" or "catalyst-activist" (two common ways to describe a common EDC stance) has spread to other cities. This is typical EDC: The service side of its reform work is both inti-mate and generalizable. "We have different models in different districts," Sandler told us. "In one, we have a pilot in a few schools and we work with the district to scale up." But this approach would not work in an-other city, she continued, where "the science supervisor told us something had to happen in every school. That meant for us—How are you going to do something in 90 schools? Spreading the money in this way meant we did not have enough dollars to do what we did in still another city—which is to have multiple teachers who serve as teacher-leaders in each school."

Whether reliant on single teacher-leaders or multiple ones, the strat-egy is based on teacher leadership, and in each instance aims to build the teacher-leaders' influence on both their principals and their peers. "The idea is that the teacher-leader will then find others who are sympathetic to the cause, interested in science, and will then develop another core group," thus mirroring the learning community initially established on the district level. EDC manages a central training mechanism that all recruits eventually end up in.

> We have conducted a very carefully planned-out professional development effort, which has taken these teacher-leaders through several years of professional development, as well as other class-room teachers. The focus is primarily concerned with curriculum decisions in the district, how to think about a curriculum frame-work within the district, how to select exemplary materials, how to then support teachers in the use of those materials. For teacher-leaders, we focus on issues around being a good facilitator, being a good teacher-leader, being better at your own practice so that you are seen in your school as providing a place where people can come and look at good science being taught. One goal of the professional development effort is to help you understand what good science is so that you can then talk about it and share it with other teachers.

So, what began as a curriculum design project, with a relative handful of teachers consulting on the design, became a major reform model in several American cities. Although adaptable to circumstance, the model is highly articulated and operates under explicit assumptions. Among them are the three explored above: that change is dependent on growth in the understanding of particular teachers, that a learning community is a good way to encourage such growth, and that by means of local leadership, understanding can be infectious. The project also assumes, in Sandler's words, "that it is not enough to work at a school site, you have to be build-ing the central office support too."

> I am happy having schools make decisions that are right for them, but they have to have support from the central office. There are just too many complexities of funding, policy changes, and how one subject overlaps and connects with another. Some things need to be coordinated.

Sandler acknowledged to us that this assumption, although widespread at EDC, is also the artifact of her long history as a consultant on district-wide change. Other of her assumptions too, although common at EDC, seem shaped by her particular experiences. For one thing, she is fiercely attentive to the etiquette that obligates outsiders who work on the inside. "We really try very hard," she told us, "not to impose change as outsiders."

> They are the ones who have the experience. We do not have the experience. We might be in a position to facilitate conversation, but it is *their* conversation. If we see that something may be going in the wrong way, just from what we know, then it is our job to provide input in a way that is sensitive and appropriate. That is where our skills come in, and I see us as pushing in ways that are both subtle and not subtle.
>
> Someone will say to me, "You write the letter to the principal," and I say, "No, it cannot be a letter from me, but do you mean should I help you figure out what should be in the letter, *your* letter? Fine."

In the shadow thus provided, Sandler gains cover for acting boldly when she thinks it appropriate to do so.

> I find myself constantly in arguments with one science supervisor, although we have a wonderful relationship. I can call her up on the phone and say, "This is ridiculous—we need to do this," but she has to want my advice. . . . We have to be seen as trusted colleagues—or, better, critical friends and problem solvers.

From the perspective of the Coalition of Essential Schools or Project Zero, Sandler's involvement in these sites' reform work might seem excessive. From other points of view, however, it seems too light.

> We work with a wonderful outside evaluation group, and sometimes they say to us, "You guys should be more forthright, be more aggressive. Tell them what they need to know." But we have a more step-back kind of way of working, though I feel we constantly balance that. Sometimes I feel we step back too far, where we could be saving them a lot of grief. But it is always the line that you walk: Would you really be saving them a lot of grief, or do they need the process part?

Meanwhile, leverage must be exerted at the right point. Jan Hawkins told us that EDC staff members acquire a sixth sense about this. Referring to one of the sites where she works, Sandler describes the process as follows:

We started working with the science supervisor, and that made sense. But then, at a certain point, we had to start working closely with the deputy superintendent of curriculum and instruction. Similarly, because of the hierarchy of who supervises principals, we now work much more closely with the supervisor of the principals. They happen to have a deputy superintendent for elementary education, and it has made a big difference getting him involved. On the other hand, we had to work with the principals first.

NETWORKING

Although a number of EDC staff members have acquired a personal reputation within the educational research community, most prefer to recycle what they learn from one project to the next without publishing it in the conventional way. Of course, the organization as a whole produces a continuous stream of writing that includes proposals, case books, curricula, teacher guides, facilitator notebooks, reports for funders, and articles for the Web. But classic theoretical writing, whether based on empirical research or reflection on experience, is much rarer at EDC. As a result, complained Ellen Wahl, the field as a whole loses access to the considerable practical knowledge of change stored up in many years of what Brian Lord terms the "streams of work" at EDC. As an example, she cited the networking instincts honed in EDC's experience in technical assistance to the Ford Foundation's Urban Math Collaboratives, which flowed into its recent experience in technical assistance to the National Science Foundation's State Systemic Initiative.

If you look at the SSI work, for example, there is a tremendous amount of activity—although it has been frustrated by the nature of the contract from NSF—but if they had their druthers, and what they do when they can is try to gather people together—same idea as the Urban Math Collaboratives—around common interests and connections. There's a real theory that flows out of the Urban Math Collaboratives—about finding natural communities and building around them. The learning communities work really comes out of that notion that you identify the places where there are already connections and reasons for association, and then you go in there and figure out what it is you can do to make those connections more robust and bring in additional resource knowledge, outside material into that in ways that people can really use it, and then engage in the discussion of use and change. I think that has flowed very strongly from the Urban Math Collaboratives work through the SSI work. I think one of the big difficulties of the SSI project was the disconnect between what funders would like to have technical assistance money be able to do—you know, the drop-leaflets-from-the-plane approach—and what EDC believes to be the long, slow process of change that comes from these kinds of associational situations.

Mark Driscoll's practice as a reformer is one reservoir for the strategic knowledge produced by the long experience of the Urban Math Collaboratives, although he has tended to eschew writing about practice in favor of practice itself. "Education reform has missionaries and theologians," he told us, and he is no theologian. "That's by way of warning," he added, "that I have not put a lot of effort into articulating this theory."

> Ideally, the sequence you would have is you would create a community in a school that develops its own perspectives and vision, articulates its values, and creates a process whereby they can continue to monitor how well they are doing vis-à-vis their vision. But finding ways to test their current reality includes looking at other people's worlds and seeing how their own measures up.

Much of what Driscoll told us of his work would echo what Morocco, Watt, Kantrov, Miller, and Sandler have said above. That is, much has had to do with establishing the first steps of the "sequence" Driscoll enumerates in his theory above—working with teams of teachers to identify and work on locally critical issues, building their professional self-image in the process, improving their capacity to communicate with each other, enhancing their leadership skills, and, of course, bolstering their understanding of mathematics. Like those of his colleagues, Driscoll's moves include personal huddling, action research, case and framework study, leveraging relationships with key leaders in a district, and efforts to scale up the teamwork of teacher-leaders until it becomes the district's whole approach to staff development. They also include moves not explicitly named by the other interviewees, but evident in a broad view of EDC's change work: attention to student assessment as a lever to affect a teacher's larger practice; visioning exercises; the examination of student work samples as a window on practice; and the naming and exploration, as in Peter Senge's (1990) work, of the mental models that tend to clutter any system.

But Driscoll spoke to us especially about the third element in his ideal sequence, namely, the step where teachers learn to look at other people's worlds. In speaking of this move, Driscoll, following the habit of other interviewees, framed it with a personal story.

I set out to be a research mathematician, and got a doctorate in mathematics, but Kent State really pushed me out into the world, and the world at that time was the Pruitt–Igoe housing projects in St. Louis where I ran into a tutoring program. There I met a group of people who wanted to start a school. It had all the romance of a Judy Garland/Mickey Rooney movie: "My dad has a barn, let's put on a dance!" Except it was, "An old lady just died and left me a warehouse, so let's put on a school!"

So, we opened this school. But what we did, 6 to 9 months before we opened the school, was to steep ourselves in philosophy—we were all smitten by Carl Rogers. In part, that was because of a consultant we had. We built the school somewhat along the lines of *Freedom to Learn*. What we chose to do was to build a model that aimed for consistency. One of the first things we did, back in 1971, was to buy a video camera and tape each other every week. Teachers would own up at the Tuesday staff meeting that they were having problems with a particular class. Then, we would tape on Wednesday and Thursday, and on Thursday afternoon, watch the tapes as a group. This was very painful, but this was the way I learned how to teach, and that and other strategies were useful in creating consistency for kids. That is all good news as far as I am concerned—it fixed in me a firm affection for consistency. But what it also did was create an orthodoxy within the school, an isolation that I think was, in the end, damaging.

Interviewer: The consistency you talk about sounds like a real bottom-up consistency, not imposed.

Driscoll: So was David Koresh's. At a certain point, consistency gets hardened, and what we did not do was inquire into how hardened it was getting.

How does a school manage to steer a course between consistency and "hardening"? For Driscoll, the answer is networking. "If you've got something underway in a school," he said, you ought to belong to a network that can help in "checking out the health" of it. His work as an agent of school change at EDC invariably has involved both helping schools to get "something underway" and networking them. Along with Brian Lord, Driscoll was one of the key "technical assisters" to the Ford Foundation-funded Urban Math Collaboratives, an effort to improve the teaching and learning of mathematics in American cities by means of the networked professional development of math teachers. The logic of the project was novel at its inception, although it has been much copied since. Giving design credit to Barbara Scott Nelson, then a program officer at Ford, Driscoll highlighted several design principles for us. One was to include others in the network besides math teachers, namely, "people in the community who also had an interest in talking about mathematics"—both person to person and by means of telecommunications. The Collaboratives were pioneers of computer conferencing. A second was to house each hub of the network at "a university, a museum, or whatever"—some facility in the particular city with a capacity to nurture a conversation among teachers and others interested in math, and also a capacity to help inspire that conversation. A third design principle was to foster cross-city ties among teachers and schools.

> It is not just a matter of broadening perspective, which is still sort of a crapshoot. If you broaden perspective in the sense of trying to see other ideas, you may or may not. But what Barbara was talking about is something fundamentally deeper, I think. Until you really are put into other people's shoes, you cannot appreciate and understand your own role.

To explain, Driscoll recounted for us the story of one group of math teachers, all from the same city, whom he encountered as they were leaving an assessment exercise during a UMC cross-city meeting. "*Those* people," one of them told Driscoll and his co-facilitator, Maria Santos, "don't have the same standards we do. They were giving 4s when we were giving 2s." Santos, then Los Angeles supervisor of mathematics and now president of the UMC, listened quietly to the teachers but offered only a noncommittal response. Later, she told Driscoll that the city they came from would make no progress in teaching mathematics until these teachers were able to understand the circumstances that teachers in other cities endure—to understand, for example, what it is like to work "in a state where the state looks over their shoulders all the time with an intensely mandated system of expectations and teacher evaluations. To know what that is like and to know how you would act is extremely important," she said. Otherwise, she implied, standards have no real roots in a teacher's practice and may represent only smugness.

MERGING PERSONAL CRAFT AND ORGANIZATIONAL STRATEGY

In the previous two sections of this chapter, relying on the words of a half-dozen experienced reformers at EDC, we highlighted school reform "moves" along a strategic continuum. For analytical purposes, we defined this continuum as ranging from small-scale to large-scale activism. However, we implied that the organization as a whole straddles the continuum and that many projects do as well. So, Molly Watt engages in intimate inquiries not just with any practitioners, but with those best positioned for leverage on larger systems; and Mark Driscoll practices large-scale intervention, but with touches of intimacy. Finally, we argued that each of the moves presented is the product of both personal and organizational influences. This last argument is relevant to a larger theme of the book: to understand how contemporary American school reform works—at least from the perspective of its nongovernmental purveyors—one must study more than the espoused theories of reform-based organizations and their strategies; one also must become acquainted with the particular craft— the theories in use—of their most seasoned agents.

How do the personal and the organizational become so entangled? One explanation involves leadership, both formal and informal. Particular practitioners of reform gain influence on their organizations over time, and others come to model their own work on these leaders' work. A second explanation, related to the first, involves enculturation. That is, partly by means of hiring preferences, and mostly by means of the influence over time of organizational norms, the practice of the reformer comes to reflect the practice of the organization.

Whatever the explanation, the phenomenon is perhaps least surprising at PZ, where a research tradition holds sway that has been heavily influenced by a few scholars. Nor is it much less surprising at CES and SDP, which are both reform *movements*. Movements depend on gestures that galvanize commitment—the words of a paramount leader or the provision of an explicit set of guiding principles. At SDP, Valerie Maholmes told us, "We all sing from the same hymnbook." However, it *is* surprising to find the phenomenon equally in evidence at EDC. In a different sense than Cathy Morocco meant when she used the expression, we found "the macro and the micro" extraordinarily well "hinged" here. Nor is this because EDC is a tightly directed organization. On the contrary, it is the least tightly organized of the four reform organizations we studied, relying on a shifting set of virtually autonomous and conceptually distinct projects. Indeed, by contrast to its ATLAS partners, EDC may seem relatively unfocused. The impression is an artifact of both its scale (with as many as 250 different projects in 1998) and its breadth (education broadly defined to include not only classrooms and schools, but policy systems, workplace learning, and community health—and not only in the United States but in at least a dozen other nations as well). Yet, wherever we looked at EDC, we sensed an overall congruence in its theory of action that is both vertical (from espoused theory to theory in use) and also horizontal (across projects—at least projects in school reform). In this concluding section of the chapter, we explore this congruence and what we take to be the commitments underlying it.

Of course, one generally can construct any number of valid interpretations of the belief system of a large and complex organization like EDC. Each interpretation is likely to have trade-offs—ours being no exception. We have perhaps traded subtlety and breadth for simplicity, and the reader can weigh the cost. If, indeed, EDC for most purposes could be defined accurately in terms of only two core commitments, as we define it below, then these would have long ago become a mainstay of its corporate voice. On the other hand, our topic here is narrower than EDC's corporate voice can ever be. We are focused on school reform, whereas EDC pursues a much broader concern based on its conception of the power of education to make lives fuller and more productive. If we had undertaken a different purpose related to this broader concern—for example, the relation of education to health or economic development—then we might have surfaced somewhat different commitments or, at least, expressed these with a different nuance. We are, moreover, constrained by our data source: the thoughts of the experienced school reformers we interviewed.

With these caveats in mind, we argue that the EDC theory in use explored earlier in this chapter has been shaped by two overlapping institutional commitments, both of them deeply rooted in EDC history. The first is a commitment to *collaborative expertise*, and the second a commitment to a *constructivist perspective on learning*.

Collaborative Expertise

Ed Campbell, former president (1970–76) and longtime chair of the board of trustees, told us that a major accomplishment of EDC's first initiative, the PSSC Physics project, was to introduce collaborative expertise into curriculum writing. "Up until then, most high school texts were written by a college professor, and if a text hit reasonably well, he had an annuity for life, revising it every 2 or 3 years." PSSC Physics changed the paradigm, Campbell told us, by bringing together diverse scholars and even film makers to work on the project. The point then was to bypass what EDC's founders saw, in Arthur Bestor's characterization, as the "interlocking directorate of professional educationists"—an "iron curtain" separating the schools from the scholarly community (Dow, 1991, p. 19). Fresh from postwar achievements like the design of a distant early warning system in defense, and a nationwide air traffic control system, Zacharias and the other scientists who founded EDC wanted to work in the same ways on educational problems. This would require a lot of paradigm breaking, including the first provision of large-scale federal funding for curriculum development and the use of a Manhattan Project or "skunks-works" research process. The former enabled, and the latter demanded, collaborative expertise.

However, the founders' style of collaborative expertise was different in an important respect from that of EDC staff at the time. The former tended to collaborate with other disciplinary experts in the development of their curricula and used practitioners only as advisors on implementation. Indeed, in the earliest EDC work, according to Peter Dow (1991), "professional educators were seen as dull-witted people who conversed in an incomprehensible 'middle language,' and were responsible for the uninspired state of American education" (p. 139). Although many system outsiders who try to make educational change today may think about insiders in this same way, they do not work at EDC. There, the idea of collaborative expertise has evolved to a quite different state, one that assigns a parity of value to disciplinary expertise, practitioner expertise, and the expertise of brokers like Cathy Morocco and Judi Sandler. Although the shift of emphasis may not have gone quite far enough in the view of CES, it is nonetheless significant. The result is that EDC has become the most even-handed of the ATLAS organizations in assigning value to diverse expertise in school reform.

According to Barbara Scott Nelson, EDC's habit of collaborating with practitioners owes much to good political instincts. Other early inclinations notwithstanding, these instincts go way back. After all, Peter Dow (1991), quoted above, also claims that EDC never seriously tried to invent "teacher-proof" curriculum despite its roots in the post-Sputnik era of curriculum design. It is true that at the start of EDC's famous Man: A Course of Study curriculum project in the late 1960s, principal investigator Jerome Bruner proposed a "Sunday Night Series of Talks to Teachers"—phonograph recordings of "lively accounts of the nature of the unit," which teachers could listen to "before starting the week"(Dow, 1991, p. 141). However, others working on the project, including a young Howard Gardner, successfully championed a more sophisticated view of teacher learning and of project collaboration with teachers. And the first evaluator of MACOS, Sylvia Farnham-Diggory, put the argument in expressly political terms, saying that more sophisticated teacher training "will probably save a dozen years of headaches in the introduction of the curriculum to the outside world" (quoted in Dow, 1991, p. 116). Although the headaches came anyway for this project, the inclination to avoid them through collaboration with teachers became a hallmark of EDC's curriculum work from then on. In the 30 years since, EDC has managed to devise numerous strategies of collaboration, and many of the moves we heard about it in our research were expressions of them.

Meanwhile, however, one thing has not changed from the earliest days. As we mentioned earlier in the chapter, Zacharias is said to have gotten involved in curriculum reform, among other reasons, because he thought the effect of the local control of curriculum stymied innovation and abetted American anti-intellectualism (Wahl, 1995). He and his colleagues intended EDC to be a supra-local advocate for change. They believed that distant expertise has an important claim to authority in educational matters. Quite apart from its now long-standing habit of honoring local expertise, EDC continues to believe as much. In its view, the groups that Ilene Kantrov, Barbara Miller, and Mark Driscoll facilitate are richer for their facilitators' critical distance; and the districts that Judi Sandler assists are better off for her nonlocal perspective.

It happens that Project Zero, the School Development Program, and the Coalition of Essential Schools also recognize implicitly the value of a national perspective in the local pursuit of school change, but they tend to mean something different by it. So, Project Zero values university-based theoretical expertise, the kind one may encounter in published research. This was once true at EDC too, when experts routinely were imported from universities for relatively brief stints. Today, however, the theoretical expertise most valued at EDC is the kind one encounters in the voices and prodding of field agents—who typically are hired as permanent staff. This is a very important difference. Nor does one find at EDC the charismatic expertise so characteristic of CES and SDP. Janet Whitla is not James Comer or Theodore Sizer, any more than she is Howard Gardner—nor does she wish to operate as they do. Indeed, although she admires these particular men, she distrusts charismatic approaches to change. Here is how she put it in an interview, in reference to a report written by an ATLAS evaluator.

Whitla: I thought she had a lot of interesting points, but when she said we all know the only change that ever really happens in education is through charismatic leaders, I thought—boy—if we count on that, we're dead ducks.

Interviewer: So, what does EDC count on instead of charisma?

Whitla: We have a very skilled staff. We have people who are skilled out there in the world. We keep trying to put all this together, to keep creating more and more sense that everyone can be a leader in some way, that everybody has to take responsibility and ownership. Everybody has to have a commitment to what they're doing, in whatever field they're in. Everybody has to feel they can keep learning. It's not in the stream of human development to do all this easily, so to keep supporting this through learning and through helping people see some of the excitement of it—that's at the heart of what everybody here believes in, why they work the way they do. But it does not lead to us having one single methodology we bring in that gets labeled, "Ah, ha! This is the EDC approach to organizational change," or "This is the EDC bandwagon we jump on."

In fact, it leads instead to a very quiet way of working, a behind-the-scenes style of collaboration. Frequently, observers do not even notice the role that EDC has played or is playing in such efforts as the Lilly Endowment's Middle Grades Improvement Project, which had a seminal impact on middle school reform; the Pew Charitable Trusts' project on systemic school reform in mid-sized cities; the Urban Math Collaboratives; the State Systemic Initiative of the National Science Foundation; or even the ATLAS Project. Janet Whitla admitted to us that "it's sometimes very frustrating to end up almost invisible," but, she added, "it's the best way we can come out. If we've done our work well, we're not the visible agents." The ones who should be noticed, she said, are "the actors who are connected and working together" as the result of EDC's quiet intervention.

Constructivist Perspective

EDC takes an inverately constructivist view of learning of any kind—whether of children or adults, whether concerning the movement of the moon as in one early curriculum project, or the design of telecommunications strategies in education. That is, from its curriculum projects to its projects in systemic reform, EDC assumes that one does not learn anything by merely being told it—in whatever sophisticated way—but rather by means of opportunities to construct in one's own understanding some meaningful approximations of it. Meanwhile, as discussed above, virtually all EDC projects are conceived as collaborations between insiders and outsiders, with one role of outsiders being to ensure that approximations do, indeed, approximate. In Cathy Morocco's words, the outsider provides "multiple levels of scaffolding" to support the construction. It is a phrase that connects EDC's own constructivist tradition to contemporary learning theory, but it also sets EDC apart from the traditions of its ATLAS partners, where the outsider is more likely to be regarded as resource or cheerleader.

By taking a constructivist perspective on learning—whether the learning of teachers or of children—EDC rejects the dominant aim of most American curriculum design, namely, to "cover" a knowledge base or field of study. Whitla told us that she cannot think of a single EDC curriculum project in which coverage in the ordinary sense was a goal. A common EDC approach instead is to use questions as pegs upon which to hang di-

verse views within a particular domain. Whitla offered the example of
EDC's Exploring Childhood project. The major organizing question, she
said, was What is a child? "Obviously," she added, "you still have to be
selective in what you bring into that, but the question allows you to dip
richly into all kinds of experiences from children's art to children's play to
children's social interactions." Another common approach is to "post-hole"
curriculum—that is, to present children or adult learners with a series of
discrete problems or cases that may collectively define some key dimension of a field but not cover the whole field.

When the field is school reform rather than childhood or biology, EDC
keeps on question-posing and post-holing. That is, unlike its ATLAS partners, particularly the School Development Program and the Coalition of
Essential Schools, EDC avoids specializing in a particular problem or view
of school reform. Each EDC project in school reform is presumed to be an
approximation, one that will be succeeded in due course by still another
approximation—other projects, other post holes. This is one of the things
that EDC staff member Nancy Ames means when she says that EDC is
permanently a multipurpose organization, whereas its ATLAS partners all
pursue more or less single purposes.

Another important consequence of a seriously constructivist approach
to learning, as applied to school reform, is that it takes time. Ed Campbell
told us that while Jerrold Zacharias was the actual founder of EDC, Jean
Piaget was its conceptual founder. He meant that the Education Development Center takes its middle name very seriously. It operates—to some
extent tacitly, and to some extent avowedly—on the assumption that
learning cannot be rushed—that it demands engagement with rich problems over time, abundant social and contextual supports, and unhurried
expectations. Moreover, it necessarily builds on previous learning, perception, and experience; even while it challenges these. To borrow a phrase
from CES, it continually requires relearning and unlearning. Consequently,
it eats up time. Within a constructivist paradigm, EDC's straddling small-
scale and large-scale interventions shows neither ambivalence nor an attempt to "cover" the field. It manifests instead the effort to combine resolve with patience. "Here's where we're headed," it offers, "but now how
are you feeling today?" Indeed, among the organizations we studied, EDC
and SDP seem the most patient. Moreover, although it is in the nature of
all activists to believe in the efficacy of their activism, EDC reformers seem
to us the least likely to believe on some tacit level that the success they
strive for may be just around the next bend.

CHAPTER 6

Becoming ATLAS

Given the differences in their histories, their clientele, and what we referred to in Chapter 1 as their developmental and political perspectives, it is not surprising that the four partner organizations of ATLAS had a somewhat uneasy partnership. Yet, some observers both within and outside the organizations expected otherwise. They hoped for a grand synthesis, a kind of summing up of 100 years of diverse theories of action. These observers chose to emphasize the evident compatibility of the organizations and their enthusiasm in coming together. They were affected as well by a widespread sense among policy makers and grant makers that some synthesis of approaches to school reform is desirable, given the formidable obstacles to its implementation, and, furthermore, that it is feasible.

In this chapter, we will explore why such a synthesis failed to emerge in ATLAS, despite the hopes and the efforts, and we also will make the claim that American school reform is none the worse for the failure. We will explain why and how the four organizations took a different step—founding a fifth organization. In a short time, this fifth organization, called ATLAS, has evolved its own theory of action, as well as its own organizational culture, clientele, and funding mechanisms. Of course, one can trace in all these aspects of ATLAS the signs of its parentage—signs that are all the more salient for the continued personal investment in ATLAS of James Comer, Howard Gardner, Ted Sizer, and Janet Whitla, and for the continuing direct involvement of EDC. However, the result is more spin-off than synthesis.

In constructing this chapter, we have drawn on the work of an ethnography team funded as part of the ATLAS Seminar, on various papers prepared for the seminar, and on the experiences of one of us—Tom Hatch—who was involved directly in the crucial first year of ATLAS development (Hatch, 1998a, 1998b, 1998c; Hatch & White, 1997). To close the story, we have drawn on the work of today's ATLAS staff.

EARLY COMMITMENTS AND PROBLEMS

In retrospect, it is hard to know whether the senior members of the ATLAS partners who put together the proposal to the New American Schools Development Corporation (NASDC) really believed in the desirability or feasibility of a grand synthesis of theories of action. However, the proposal itself seems unequivocal in this regard.

> There would be no point in joining forces if we were simply to add, say, the CES's Nine Principles to the SDP's Six Pathways. What legitimizes and energizes our collaboration is the prospect of creating a new approach to education that is greater than, and different from, anything that we can accomplish alone. (Proposal to NASDC, 1991, p. 4)

Drawing on rhetoric from all four partners, the proposal outlined a vision of students and teachers working "together on problems and issues of significance within and outside of school," developing "habits of mind, heart, and work . . . within a context of standards valued by families and by the scholarly disciplines" (p. 1). This vision was to become operational in a "pathway" of schools (one high school and at least one elementary and middle school in its feeder pattern). The partners argued in the proposal that the development of such pathways requires simultaneous changes in a number of different aspects of ordinary schooling. Among these are its organization and management, the quality of its learning environments, the nature of its assessment system, the character of its professional development practices, the extent and manner of its community involvement, and its use of technology. Needed too are changes in any number of district policies that bear on individual schools and the nature of their relationship with each other. ATLAS proposed to work with four districts as collaborators in the designing work. The sites later chosen were Gorham, Maine; Lancaster, Pennsylvania; Norfolk, Virginia; and Prince George's County, Maryland (although Lancaster withdrew early). The proposal suggested that the design to be developed would be one flexible enough to take on a somewhat different character in each of the designing sites. Still, the proposal forecast some commonalities of design: site-based planning at the school level and management teams involving parents as partners; inquiry-based, hands-on curricula; and assessment systems involving the use of portfolios and exhibitions. The proposal had an additive bias—as if the theories of action of the four partners might be simply added on to each other, as if they were in all respects commensurate, and as if the partners' usual theories in use were unlikely on occasion to cancel each other out.

Once funded, the partners established an ATLAS staff comprising, first of all, members of the four organizations. New staff members also were hired, but the hires were considered staff of their "home organizations" as well as of ATLAS. A senior member of each organization jointly directed the project, with CES serving as the primary contractor and center of financial operations.

Challenges surfaced quickly in the new organization. Decision making and product development were slower than anticipated. Discussions among ATLAS staff often dragged on without resolution, and materials had to be revised numerous times. Meanwhile, even as ATLAS was struggling to become a genuinely collaborative enterprise of the four partners, it actually was becoming from the perspective of the partners an independent entity with its own unique structures and culture. This was true even from the perspective of CES, where the ATLAS office was housed. The phenomenon is quite understandable: The ATLAS staff simply had too much to do to get its new and complicated initiative off the ground, without also spending time and energy explaining the initiative to its "home" colleagues.

In the end, issues over how to direct and manage the project led to a major reorganization after only a few months. A management team that included a single project director and two other senior staff in a more hierarchical arrangement replaced the four co-directors. None of the members of this new management team had worked for any of the partner organizations prior to ATLAS. The reshuffling proved traumatic—not only for the young ATLAS organization itself, but for the home organizations also. Then, at the end of the first year, ATLAS was reconfigured again. This time—reflecting what actually had occurred in terms of organizational culture—it was organized as an independent entity. The office moved to EDC, whose own culture is conducive to independent projects, and the ATLAS staff no longer functioned in any practical sense as home organization staff also (Fanning, Muncey, & White, 1994).

DIFFERENT THEORIES OF ACTION AT WORK

Below the surface of the struggle to become ATLAS lay a theoretical problem. The principles, strategies, and moves of the organizations that formed ATLAS—and that have been analyzed in the previous chapters of this book—reflect different theories of action. The differences among them are not merely differences of rhetoric and tactics such as might be resolved by a clever committee. They are instead differences in the *conception* of reform, involving dynamic, multidimensional systems of belief and practice.

In Chapter 1, citing Donald Schön, we accounted for these differences by means of an analytical structure involving three levels: espoused theory, design theory, and theory in use.

Being in its early days an unassimilated coalition, ATLAS really "held" these three levels of its theory of action times four. So, for example, the espoused theory of ATLAS as outlined in its proposal to NASDC was really four theories added together, rather than one coherent theory.[1] The first design elements followed suit. And, of course, in their work with the ATLAS sites, the ATLAS staff tended naturally to practice its moves as it might have practiced them within the respective home organizations. That is, theory in use was also unassimilated. Thus, there were many theories of action in play during the ATLAS planning year.

Meanwhile, there was hardly any time to reflect on all this difference. NASDC had its own theory of action, which involved the rapid development and implementation of a range of new designs for schools. To ensure rapidity, NASDC required ATLAS to produce 44 deliverables in the first year (such as technology plans, lists of resources, and summaries of work in the sites). Meanwhile, the ATLAS staff, racing furiously to meet the quarterly deadlines for deliverables, also had to deal with the constant threat that if the ATLAS design was not satisfactorily completed in the first year—or if NASDC failed to raise enough money—the project would not be re-funded.

Schön's analytical framework helps us to discern the heart of the problem of becoming ATLAS. This was a complex undertaking. It involved not only what people from four belief-driven organizations said about their purpose—with all its implicit inconsistencies and disagreements. It also involved what they chose to emphasize in their contributions to the designing work, in accord with their avowed as well as tacit assumptions about how one best designs for change. Finally, it involved what they actually did in working with each other and with their first school partners in tense and difficult circumstances. The reader who has read the previous chapters of this book knows that the beliefs underpinning the ATLAS partner organizations are far from casual, that the strategies the organizations employ are hard-won, and that the moves its activists favor are in many cases intuitively based. All these beliefs, strategies, and moves were put at risk within ATLAS—given the expectation of a grand synthesis. The possibility that the grand synthesis might end up benefiting American schools in the way that NASDC imagined, was in every practical and emotional sense a necessarily secondary consideration. Meanwhile, there was so little time for the reflection, experimentation, and development of relationships and new ideas needed to create a whole greater than the sum of its parts. Given these circumstances, the fact that

ATLAS emerged at all—and that it survives today—seems in retrospect a miracle.

During the first 2 years of ATLAS, the diverse theories of action at play came into conflict within a number of arenas. Differences at the level of espoused theory were in most cases, although not all, the easiest to handle. So long as the ATLAS official positions and publications did not directly contradict the stated goals and values of the four organizations, differences at this level usually could be finessed—often by operating at a level of abstraction that blurred troublesome distinctions. The four ATLAS leaders—that is, Comer, Gardner, Sizer, and Whitla—were particularly careful in their discussions and public presentations to articulate the espoused theories of their organizations in ways that emphasized compatibility and complementarity. They were not disingenuous in this regard. In fact, they appreciated what they were learning from each other's company and were on most occasions one step removed from having to accommodate the new learning within actual designs for schools. From such a perspective, compatibility and complementarity seem more salient than difference.

Problems erupted mostly when choices had to be made about what materials to create, about how to allocate time, money, and attention in order to support the work of the sites, and about what staff should do. These were all matters of design theory and theory in use. It was simply not possible for the staff to create materials or act in ways that were entirely consistent with the design theories and theories in use of all four organizations at the same time—particularly given constraints on resources and the fierce NASDC timetable. Differences especially mattered when the staff considered the most basic issues of school reform: How to begin the work and with whom? What kind of curriculum to create? What kind of supports to provide for adult and organizational development (Hatch, 1998a)?

How to Begin?

ATLAS believes, as a matter of espoused theory, that school reform is both multifaceted and necessarily collaborative—that many different aspects of schooling need to change at once and that the change cannot be sustained without the involvement of all members of the school community. At this level of abstraction, all four of its parent organizations agree. At a practical level, however, the four organizations start the process differently. SDP, for example, believes that the first step is to establish consensus among all stakeholders in the school community. "Rallying the whole village" is not just a slogan at SDP, but a focus of training and resource development. By contrast, the other partners tend to begin more narrowly. They focus especially on the school's professional staff. They seek variously to support the development of teachers' own visions for change, to equip them with new ideas about school design or the subjects they teach, to provide them new materials for teaching, or to coax them to try out new designs for teaching and learning.

In ATLAS, the question of how to begin came down to whether each ATLAS site should focus on building a consensus for change first, or on introducing specific innovations first and going for consensus later. Even the ATLAS leaders evinced some disagreement here. For example, Comer often spoke about the need for building relationships before anything else, and he promoted the role of organization and management structures in doing that. For his part, Sizer often emphasized that if the school structures that contributed to high student–teacher ratios did not change, nothing else could change. These positions were not offered as counterpoint, however. In fact, Sizer and Comer frequently pronounced their support for each other's position.

However, when it came time for the ATLAS staff to make design decisions, as we will see below, conflict was less easily sidestepped. For example, tensions were evident in discussions during the first year about the design of a 1-week Summer Institute for the ATLAS sites (Fanning, Muncey, & White, 1994). On the one hand, some staff felt that the development of the School Planning and Management Teams (SPMTs) and the provision of skills needed to facilitate conversations and come to consensus should be the primary focus of this institute. They argued that equipping the sites with these teams fast, and ensuring that the teams had the skills they needed, would provide the best possible basis on which to develop and put in place the other elements of the ATLAS design. Other staff, by contrast, wanted to focus the first Summer Institute on the development of the kind of authentic learning activities touted in the NASDC proposal. They worried that unless ATLAS teachers had an early opportunity to experience and explore such learning activities, all the rest of the ATLAS development would be stunted. Some argued that the whole institute should be carried out in ways consistent with authentic teaching and learning, with participants pursuing projects guided by essential questions and demonstrating in the end what they had learned through exhibitions.

Eventually, the institute planners agreed to split the difference and to feature both training for the SPMTs and also experience in authentic learning activities. But the basic tension reappeared over the question of whom to invite to the institute and about how much time to dedicate to particular activities. The ATLAS staff members who wanted to use the institute to build site teams naturally wanted to invite parents, administrators, and other staff, as well as teachers. But the ATLAS staff members who especially wanted to feature authentic learning, and who hoped for maximal impact, had in mind an institute composed largely of teachers. Within budget constraints, it was impossible to accommodate both visions.

Such disagreements over where and how to begin were played out not only in the design of activities and materials, but also in the preparation of deliverables to NASDC. And they also were played out in the design sites. For example, in the second year of the project, the two sites that had some previous association with SDP moved ahead by creating SPMTs. However, the third site, which had a previous PZ connection, avoided the development of SPMTs. This reflected a larger caution there with respect to community involvement in reform.

> Although [the site] was committed to educating parents and community members about, and including them in, the change process, the district initially adopted a cautious approach toward informing the wider community about ATLAS because of concern about the possible negative reactions from community members who had not been supportive of the schools and reform efforts in the past. Because the design teams would include a variety of stakeholders, there was also concern about how the work of the teams might proceed. Consequently, the site team and administrators worked in a "very reflective and slow-paced manner," tackling issues and making agreements amongst themselves before communicating with and involving a larger audience. (White, Fanning, & Muncey, 1995, p. 123)

In this case, therefore, the theory in use at one of the sites conflicted with the espoused theory and official design theory of ATLAS. But, reflecting the theories of action of their home organizations, some ATLAS staff members disagreed over whether this was a problem. Indeed, to some, this site's manifest efforts to invest first in curriculum and assessment redesign were likely to lead to greater and faster progress. To other staff members, however, the same efforts seemed likely—absent the community involvement—to lead to quicker resistance.

The same tension existed with respect to the perceived urgency in reducing student–teacher ratios in the schools. For some ATLAS staff members, the prevailing ratios and implicated schedules in the partner schools were not key problems, while for others they were crucial ones. Numerous discussions were held among the interested parties as to whether reduction of teacher–student ratios was a "nonnegotiable" starting condition for "break the mold" school reform, or one of its later targets. As a result of disagreement on this point, the expectations relayed to the sites were shaped largely by the organizational background and theories in use of the ATLAS staff designated as site liaisons.

What Should ATLAS Students Learn?

The partners' approaches to curriculum reflect both their clearest agreements and their most obvious disagreements. These four reform organizations and their leaders have been among the strongest advocates of learning experiences that recognize and build upon the needs and interests of individual children. Moreover, each of the organizations endorses the idea that individual children learn best when teachers know them and care for them, and when schools collaborate with others to ensure that the children's basic social and health needs are met. Finally, the organizations agree on the need for teachers to feel some ownership of the curriculum they teach.

At the same time, there are significant differences among the organizations in terms of the kind of curriculum they tend to develop and why. These differences reflect deeper differences in their theories of action. CES promotes interdisciplinary curriculum; EDC and PZ have developed some interdisciplinary curricula but also focus primarily on promoting deep learning of concepts in specific disciplines. For its part, SDP has shown a greater interest than the other organizations in curricula that focus directly on the skills measured in standardized tests. At CES, the design of interdisciplinary curricula and exhibitions and the use of essential questions are critical strategies in reorganizing the school. At EDC and PZ, a focus on disciplinary learning goals and the deepening of disciplinary understanding is a key strategy in building professional capacity for reform. And at SDP, the alignment of curricula with standardized tests and other representations of community standards is a key part of bringing school and community together (Rogers, 1996).

Although some ATLAS associates wondered why ATLAS couldn't have disciplinary *and* interdisciplinary curricula, or focus on standardized tests *and* deep disciplinary content, the truth is that each of the organizations to some extent had built its theory of action in opposition to one side or the other of these dualities. The differences were particularly evident in the meetings and memos of the ATLAS leaders, with Sizer being the most passionate advocate of an interdisciplinary perspective and Gardner the most vocal in promoting a disciplinary position. Essentially, Gardner argued that robust understandings of important phenomena and concepts depend on the study of disciplines like history, the natural sciences, and mathematics. In most school subjects, by contrast, students often are presented collections of facts that fail to reflect the methods, concepts, and key issues central to development and progress in the disciplines and professions. Interdisciplinary curricula typically do no better, he and Veronica Boix-Mansilla argued in a 1994 paper. Sizer, who debated Gardner and

Boix-Mansilla in several meetings of the ATLAS Seminar, agreed with their concerns about the traditional subjects taught in school, but was not convinced, he said, that disciplinary approaches of the kind they advocated would result in much improvement. He claimed that the disciplines as epistemological conventions have limited usefulness in school and that they fragment and compartmentalize knowledge and seriously constrain teachers' abilities to connect with the way children perceive the world. Responding to a draft of the Gardner and Boix-Mansilla paper, Sizer (1992b) had this to say:

> We can take a lot of time worrying this epistemological bone and thereby emerge with some tight distinctions, ones that we find satisfactory and, indeed, necessary for our own personal quests for understanding. However, the work of kids (at whatever tender or less tender stage of intellectual development) calls first for careful, but nonetheless gross distinctions. We paralyze them with a sort of complexity (however worthy and appropriate) which is the meat and drink of mature minds. (p. 2)

Such differences in the organizations' espoused views of curriculum played out as well in the discussions among the first ATLAS staff about the kinds of materials to develop and the kind of advice to offer sites. For example, there was a protracted debate about the nature of the program's "standards," or statements of targeted outcomes for students. An initial paper focused broadly on the development of habits and understandings without mentioning particular disciplines or specifying particular skills that students in ATLAS schools should develop (Lear, 1993). Some staff members dissented from the view represented in this paper, wondering how a concentration on such broad habits and understandings could help students who were struggling to learn to read and calculate. They argued, instead, for a "common core" of skills, habits, and understandings that articulated what all ATLAS students should know and be able to do. To this end, one member of the ATLAS Assessments and Standards Task Force offered a revision of the original paper that articulated a long list of essential skills and understandings. The resulting debate continued for 2 years.

Differences in the ATLAS partners' points of view about what to teach in an ATLAS school were also evident in discussions about the use of standardized tests. At the level of design theory, ATLAS favored policy waivers from such tests on the grounds that they are inimical to the kinds of authentic learning experiences ATLAS promotes. But at the level of theory in use, some ATLAS staff members worried that exemptions from standardized tests would prevent ATLAS schools from ensuring that their students were developing the skills they needed to succeed in the wider society. In the end, decisions about whether to pursue policy waivers were left up to each site, advised by the particular ATLAS staff member serving as site liaison. Some did pursue waivers, and some did not.

How to Support ATLAS Reform?

The early ATLAS debates about how to begin reform, and about the nature of the ATLAS curriculum, were tied to a third point of contention—namely, how much support to provide ATLAS schools and teachers, and what kind of support. Like the ATLAS partners, ATLAS itself promoted local ownership of reform, believing that reform depends ultimately on local leadership and local creative action. But the idea entails a practical dilemma. On the one hand, too much guidance or direction from the outside—in this case, from ATLAS or its agents—can sap the development of local ownership. On the other hand, not enough can deprive locals of exactly the learning opportunities and access to expertise they need to sustain ownership. As the reader will recall from the previous chapters, all four partners wrestle knowingly with this dilemma. On the other hand, they have tended to evolve different rules of thumb for managing it. Both SDP and EDC function on the support-heavy side of the continuum. They tend to rely on detailed training mechanisms, defined expectations for implementation of reforms, and the provision of detailed resource materials. CES and PZ, by contrast, operate on quite the other side of the continuum. They provide broad frameworks like the Common Principles or the theory of multiple intelligences, and then, by various means, offer practitioners opportunities to explore what the frameworks mean and to experiment with these meanings.

Like the other differences we discussed above, this one too got passed on to ATLAS. It figured especially in an ATLAS debate about the value and contents of a memorandum of understanding (MOU) as a support for sites. The idea was that ATLAS and each of its sites might confirm their commitments to one another in writing, thus offering the sites the chance to state what supports they felt were needed, and offering ATLAS the opportunity to lay out its sense of the "nonnegotiables" of ATLAS reform. Some ATLAS staff felt that this set of nonnegotiables might constitute a kind of scaffold for site development. Other staff felt that such a formal mechanism would introduce an inappropriate tone into the partnership, and that it also would preclude an experimental attitude toward the questions that still troubled ATLAS—settling them prematurely. Should districts be asked, for example, to commit to establishing SPMTs, to initiate block scheduling, to lower student–teacher ratios?

Eventually, the MOU strategy was adopted as a design component and its contents spelled out. A significant portion of the second ATLAS Summer Institute was then spent introducing the MOU to site teams and preparing them to get their districts to sign it. But, predictably, the response to the MOU from the site teams was mixed and, in the end, not all sites employed the strategy (White, Fanning, & Muncey, 1995).

Questions about the appropriate character of support for implementation were also at the heart of a long dispute about professional development activities for teachers. Whether conducted centrally by ATLAS staff—as in the Summer Institutes—or locally by liaisons and district personnel, should such activities be designed in a relatively open way, or in a more directive one? Some ATLAS staff worried that too much structure and direction would dishonor teachers' own expertise and also cheat them of opportunities for building capacity to sustain the reform. Others worried that too much open-endedness in these activities would prove frustrating for teachers ready to move and also result in great inefficiencies as the teachers struggled to discover on their own some practices and insights that more knowledgeable reformers simply might have shared with them. There were heated exchanges on this issue, and these tended to spill over into the home organizations. So, for example, some ATLAS activities that PZ and EDC staff felt were quite sensitive to the needs and concerns of teachers were viewed by some CES staff as attempts to "teacher-proof" the designs. Tensions over language surfaced too. Terms like "scaffolding" and "intervention"—which commonly were employed at PZ and EDC in reference to professional development work—grated on CES ears (Krechevsky & Morocco, 1996).

One other area where different perspectives surfaced on the nature and extent of ATLAS support concerned curriculum design. Here the question was whether ATLAS should encourage sites to adopt curriculum already designed and available from EDC, and that seemed highly compatible with the ATLAS vision of authentic learning communities, or whether it instead should encourage and help sites to develop their own curricula—as CES tended to do in its work with member schools. In its second year, ATLAS settled the question for itself by designing a Curriculum Planning Framework as a tool for site-based curriculum design. But by this time, the ATLAS staff was a second staff, whose members felt little or no allegiance to the home organizations. Thus its "resolution" of the question actually added to the centrifugal forces drawing the overall partnership apart—those forces that eventually resulted in a distinctly separate and fifth organization named ATLAS. For some staff of the partner organizations, this framework became symbolic of what they took to be the ponderous nature of ATLAS—for example, asking teachers to plan curriculum not only with CES "essential questions" in mind, but also with PZ "generative ideas." Others continued to believe that asking ATLAS teachers to spend a lot of time in curriculum planning simply made no sense, given the availability—particularly through the EDC connection—of good curriculum materials and professional development opportunities (White, Muncey, & Fanning, 1998).

CONSTRAINTS ON SYNTHESIS

In seeking partners who had had success in complementary areas of school reform, the four ATLAS partners may well have been more interested in supplementing their current work than in seeking a basis to transform it. In this conception of ATLAS, the project was a temporary laboratory supported jointly, within which each of the four partners could enhance its own perspective without endangering its essentially separate character. Thus the first condition constraining synthesis may well have been reluctance by the parties concerned, reluctance founded on reasonable interpretations of what their non-ATLAS commitments demanded of them. In judging whether it was good or bad that ATLAS failed to generate a grand synthesis, one has to weigh the value of synthesis against the likelihood of the partners' temporary loss of capacity to do their pressing work. Of course, the question now is moot. That is, the partners learned some things through ATLAS but staved off synthesis, and, in the process, they created yet another organization to join them in a field that is plenty big enough for all five.

In this section of the chapter, however, we put aside the mootness of the question in order to consider what would have been needed in order to create an integration of the partners' theories of action—that is, in addition to the partners' genuine willingness. We do so in the interest of exploring larger questions of the likelihood and desirability of grand syntheses in American school reform. At the heart of our inquiry is the question of whether one should strive for such levels of rationality in a complex field like American school reform, or expect the field, instead, to be full of inevitably partial strategies that can never be made fully compatible.

But, presuming that they want to and that they can, *where* might four organizations with 100 years of collective knowledge work on synthesizing this knowledge? The ATLAS partners chose two distinct places: an organization with a design mission, and a seminar with a research mission.

ATLAS the Organization

One way to understand the constraints on synthesis associated with ATLAS the organization is to focus on the NASDC demands. The New American Schools Development Corporation set out to support the development of school designs that "break the mold," that is, ones that depart radically from late-twentieth-century school design and in the process make up for its perceived shortcomings. However, there was a lack of congruence between NASDC's espoused theory and its design theory. To "break the mold," the design teams would have had to engage in some major exploration of problems with the mold, of feasible ways to break it, and of options to replace it. But NASDC specifically forbade any design teams from using NASDC funds on research activities. Moreover, as we suggested above, the pace of NASDC expectations militated even against reflective inquiry. Although NASDC (later NAS) softened these requirements somewhat over the years, it initially expected the design teams to develop new break-the-mold school designs in a single year, implement them in test sites the following 2 years, and then begin general dissemination in the fourth year. In imposing these conditions, NASDC also implicitly imposed its own theory of how one breaks the mold, namely, by coming up quickly with a better idea and selling the idea rapidly to a sufficient number of customers.

Organization and management theorists argue that the kinds of procedures NASDC employed encourage organizations to exploit, expand, or build on already successful practices, rather than develop new ones (Hatch, 1998c; Leventhal & March, 1993; March, 1991). This is surely not a bad thing. In many cases, exploitation is much less risky and often more profitable than exploration. On the other hand, it usually does not break molds. Moreover, the NASDC design conflicted with its espoused theory in other ways. For example, although NASDC encouraged designs to reach for "world-class standards" and to develop and use alternative assessments, it evaluated the designs partly on the basis of their effectiveness in raising students' test scores. Indeed, in later years, NASDC increased the pressures to focus on approaches that might improve standardized test performance by linking the continued funding of the design teams to their ability to attract schools and districts willing to pay for the use of the designs. Since most schools and districts have to show improvements on conventional measures, the fee-for-service design created still further disincentives for the broad exploration of alternative approaches to accountability. The evaluation of NASDC conducted by RAND concluded that those design teams that demonstrated the potential to improve student achievement most quickly (as measured by standardized tests) tended to have an existing and established team (before NASDC funding), focused most directly on core academic subjects like reading and math, and centered on the fewest numbers of schools and grade levels (Bodilly, 1996). Teams like ATLAS, which tried to create a new staff or organization, sought to work with larger numbers of schools, designed for high schools as well as elementary schools, and focused on many aspects of schooling rather than just the core academic subjects linked most closely to standardized test performance, tended to be less successful (Bodilly, 1996; Stringfield, Ross, & Smith, 1996).

In hoping for a grand synthesis in ATLAS of four experienced reform groups, and in expecting it to occur quickly, NASDC seriously underestimated what such a synthesis requires. On the other hand, what it requires—in terms of time and resources and organizational flux—seems incompatible with the NASDC theory of action. NASDC may have been conceived originally as an instrument of radical school redesign, but as a consequence of its own design theory, it evolved into an instrument of school improvement instead (Hatch, 1998c). This is hardly an unhappy outcome, particularly inasmuch as it has left unaffected (in the case of ATLAS) its partners' capacity to keep working toward something bigger.

A second way to assess the constraints on synthesis within ATLAS the organization is to consider the issue of staff turnover. All of the tensions we explore above, and they are the predictable tensions associated with an effort to achieve a synthesis of deeply held beliefs, took their toll on the ATLAS staff (White, Fanning, & Muncey, 1998). The first to go were the senior staff members selected by the partnership organizations to launch ATLAS. After the first year, they had either returned to the partner organizations or in some cases left the scene entirely. Most of their junior colleagues left at about the same time. After the third year, a similarly large turnover occurred again, in connection with a change of directors. To this day, of those who have served in leadership positions within ATLAS, only the four original co-directors of the project worked in one of the partner organizations before they began their work with ATLAS.

Meanwhile, even as the ATLAS staff was changing, the people with whom the staff worked also were changing constantly. In two of the three sites, almost half of the ATLAS facilitators changed every year. Principals in over half of the ATLAS schools changed within the first 3 years, and all the superintendents have changed by now. Because of this turnover, time that might have been spent building on experiences and deepening joint work was spent instead on forging relationships and communicating basic information. As the four ATLAS partners know well from their experience apart from ATLAS, these circumstances are simply part of the ordinary terrain of American schooling. They do not reflect badly on ATLAS or on its pilot sites, but they necessarily constrain efforts to work reflectively on a grand theory of action.

Finally, three of the four ATLAS partner organizations—the ones built on a model of charismatic leadership—also have begun to undergo predictable shifts in leadership. At SDP, Ed Joyner has assumed oversight for daily operations as Executive Director. Although Ted Sizer remains Chairman of CES, he has handed over policy-making authority to a National Congress elected by member schools, which in turn has selected Amy Gerstein as Executive Director. In addition, many of the original CES staff members with whom ATLAS worked have either moved to the Annenberg Institute for School Reform at Brown (which in turn has become increasingly distant from CES) or left Brown entirely. Finally, as early as the first year of ATLAS, Howard Gardner began discussing with the PZ staff his intention to remove himself gradually from the direct management of PZ's operations. In such circumstances, these partner organizations have had to tend to their own organizational issues, while ATLAS as a separate organization has had to tend to itself. Predictably, this has strengthened its independence and at the same time weakened its effectiveness as synthesizer. The only oddity in the ATLAS experience in this regard may be the fact that anyone associated with it expected anything different to happen.

ATLAS the Seminar

As we stated above, however, the ATLAS partnership relied on more than ATLAS itself to work out the synthesis it promised. There was also the ATLAS Seminar. The Seminar was designed to provide all the reflective space that ATLAS the organization by design lacked. The very existence of this book is evidence of its success in this regard. However, reflection may well lead to deeper understanding plus *more* rather than less distinctiveness. Rather than facilitate synthesis, reflection may clarify reasons to avoid it.

As a research enterprise, ATLAS the seminar was itself complicated by theoretical differences among the partners. Underlying these differences were questions about whose expertise, whose perspective, and whose voice matter most in the generation of new knowledge about school reform. In Chapter 1 of this book, we recounted Tom Hatch's surprise as a researcher to discover that CES was initially more concerned about whether practitioners would attend the Seminar than about what topics the Seminar would take up. Yet neither the question of Seminar identity raised by the CES concern and by Hatch's surprise, nor innumerable other Seminar questions, were ever resolved to any of the partner organizations' complete satisfaction—including the question of what topics to take up and of how to treat them.

Differences among the partners in their methodological habits also played some part in the Seminar. At SDP, research has tended to follow social science norms; at CES, it has tended to entail experimental methods involving collaborative action research; at PZ, it has meant small-scale clinical research; at EDC, it has nearly always been joined to development work as in classic research and development. Moreover, there is the difference in stance. SDP and CES are both advocacy organizations where research is focused on questions of implementation and of efficacy. PZ, by contrast, is a research organization above all, whose mission goes well beyond testing the implementation and efficacy of particular reform programs. Finally, EDC is a massive engine of applied research—yet again a different kind of creature. To meld together such diverse habits and assumptions would, of course, have taken much resolve in terms of acknowledging differences, bracketing assumptions, and risking fundamental reorientation by all the parties. At the least, it would have taken lots of frank talk. As the outside consultants who served as a review team for the ATLAS Seminar suggested, however, many discussions within the seminar could not get "beyond politeness" (ATLAS Seminar, 1995).

Integrating Organization and Seminar

Looking back, most ATLAS members agree that it would have made more sense to begin by spending more time learning about one another and developing the personal relationships and new ideas that could provide a foundation for a partnership and joint work in schools. But NASDC offered an opportunity and a challenge to move ahead that were too tempting to ignore. Beyond its beginnings, however, there were a number of other factors that made it difficult to integrate the work of ATLAS the organization and ATLAS the seminar. First of all, the NASDC timeline, demands for deliverables, and the injunction on research hovered over ATLAS the reform organization throughout the project. Second, there was no agreement among Seminar members about how directly to involve itself with ATLAS in its sites. Some thought that the ATLAS design had papered over differences among the partners and that it was the business of the Seminar to uncover these differences, which meant imagining an ATLAS different from the one being enacted in the sites.[2] And there were also questions among the ATLAS–NASDC members about how useful a research enterprise like the Seminar could be in dealing with the day-to-day work in the sites. Third, with separate missions, staffing, and funding, coordinating the ideas and activities of ATLAS–NASDC and the Seminar

was no easier than coordinating the school reform efforts of the four partner organizations. For these reasons, ATLAS did its synthesizing work in
two places rather than one, and the two entities went about their business relatively independently, mimicking the tendency throughout American education for practice and research to proceed in parallel play.

ATLAS TODAY

ATLAS today is an independent, fee-for-service school reform project. It
offers the districts and schools that are its clients one of the New American School designs,[3] tested by experience in the original ATLAS sites, and
honed by the reflective practice over the years of dozens of ATLAS staff
and consultants. To help those who would adopt this design, ATLAS relies
on a lean staff based at EDC in Newton, Massachusetts. The staff is composed of a Project Director, an Associate Director, a site-developer, a facilitator, a communications assistant, and two administrative assistants. ATLAS
relies also on three field-based consultants, who work closely with developing sites. At the moment, there are developing pathways in nine different communities including Philadelphia; Florida's Broward County;
Memphis, Tennessee; Everett and Seattle, Washington; Gorham, Maine;
Prince George County, Maryland, and Norfolk, Virginia.

ATLAS today has its own theory of action, the product of its own experience and its connection to New American Schools. It is one with roots
in the reform theories of the ATLAS parent organizations, but is full as
well of novel designs and practices. Of the parent organizations, all but
EDC—where ATLAS is housed—are more distant now from their offspring,
although James Comer, Ted Sizer, and Howard Gardner continue to be
involved. The present Director, Linda Gerstle, joined ATLAS in 1994—fresh
from an effort to build a state-level network of Accelerated Schools. Since
then, she has managed the remarkable transformation of ATLAS from a
grant-funded partnership of other reform entities to a viable reform entity in its own right.

The ATLAS theory of action continues to emphasize the development
of "pathways" across the ordinarily disconnected levels of schooling from
kindergarten to high school graduation. A pathway is characterized by
what ATLAS calls a continuously authentic and personalized learning
environment, and by a broad and inclusive school community. ATLAS
believes that pathways depend on sustained professional development and
supportive organization and management structures.

The ATLAS design has undergone considerable development during
Gerstle's tenure and under the influence of the New American Schools

scale-up phase. It relies especially today on two change mechanisms that it lacked in the beginning—an exploration process during which prospective ATLAS sites consider the implications of deep involvement, and teacher study groups that focus on making the pathway real.

ATLAS developed its exploration process in response to the New American Schools effort to recruit prospective sites for all its partners' school designs. Clearly these sites needed some opportunity—beyond brochures or other pitches—to find out if ATLAS was right for them. As Linda Gerstle put it, "It can't be us coming to sell it, it has to be you in your district who understand how it can help you, how it helps your kids, your community—you advocating for that from within." She added, "An understanding upfront of what the accountability issues are, is also critical. How do you get your ducks in a row, so to speak? What *are* the ducks and what order do they need to be in?" Called "Charting the Course," the exploration process lasts for 6 months, during which a group of key stakeholders from the district identifies needs and considers how these may match what ATLAS can provide. This stakeholders' group typically includes the superintendent, parents and other community members, principals, and teachers. Their exploration begins with a 2-day retreat facilitated by an ATLAS staff member, and continues with a series of activities—some 50 hours' worth—involving the collection and analysis of district data, including student work samples. It concludes with a data-based discussion of whether making a further commitment to ATLAS makes sense. Its purpose goes beyond exploring ATLAS, however, according to Gerstle. Her hope is that the process may help create an ongoing leadership group within each school, as well as a collective sense of district assets and challenges. These, she says, will serve the district well, whether it decides to work more with ATLAS or not.

The other central strategy that is part of the ATLAS design today is the Study Group Process. The Study Group Process grew out of ATLAS work with several Memphis sites, and it involves the whole school faculty in regular, focused discussions around classroom practice and schooling. "That's where we are beginning to develop a common language and a common understanding of one another," Gerstle told us. "We're testing all our common assumptions and beliefs in the study groups." As in the exploration process, the work begins with a retreat, facilitated by ATLAS. Each school establishes a "focus team" of volunteers who participate in the retreat and who learn how to serve as facilitators who can guide and support the study groups on each campus in the pathway.

Through the regular meetings, the study groups not only help to build a collegial environment; they also provide an arena in which teachers can examine ATLAS practices such as Teaching for Understanding. In order to support these efforts, ATLAS consultants like Carlene Murphy meet regularly with the facilitators and discuss how the facilitators can help the groups move forward. Key to the process, Gerstle emphasizes, is to start where teachers are—to introduce the concept of teaching for understanding or to pursue issues of mathematics or other issues when they come up naturally within the conversation. As Gerstle puts it, "If the teachers [in the study groups] don't start with math, they're going to get there. If you let them start where they are, as long as each one of them has to take responsibility for relating it back directly to what they are going to do in their classroom, they are going to get to math very quickly."

Another important move is to help the study groups focus directly on data—everything from student work to attendance rates, numbers of disciplinary actions, and frequency of usage of library books or computers. To that end, ATLAS has created several booklets and tools that provide guidelines for looking at student work and examples of student work that can serve as the focus for discussions. Finally, the members of ATLAS make sure that the issues that arise in study group conversations are taken to School Planning and Management Teams or other decision-making bodies so that appropriate actions can be taken.

Beyond the impact of the study groups on individual schools, the process is designed to have an impact throughout the pathway by surfacing issues of common concern. Thus, at the pathway level, ATLAS convenes representatives of each school's study groups, and they discuss the issues arising on their own campuses, identify common concerns, and develop action plans to address them. In this way, one pathway in Seattle identified the improvement of students' writing as a central concern, and developed a pathway-wide approach to the problem.

These new designs show traces of influence by the founding ATLAS partners. For example, the exploration process is similar to processes that both SDP and CES employ. The emphasis on data including student work samples shows the influence of PZ. The study group shows the influence of Cathy Morocco at EDC, who advised the first ATLAS experiment with study groups in a number of Memphis schools. Yet when Gerstle talks about these strategies and how they have evolved, she is more likely to refer to what ATLAS has learned from its own experience and to the lessons learned by consultant Carlene Murphy, who worked with similar study groups long before she came to ATLAS. Similarly, when Gerstle speaks of the ATLAS efforts to ground both the exploration and the Study Group Process in data collection and analysis, she draws as much on her previous work with the Accelerated Schools Project as on the traditions at PZ or SDP.

The reasons are not hard to understand. Gerstle was not at ATLAS when the partners were most involved, and the fruits of their involvement have long since been subsumed within the theory of action of the new and independent ATLAS. We say "long since" in recognition of the fact that "long since" may involve little more than 2 or 3 years within the fast-paced world of school reform—where most grants last only about that long, and many staff come and go in as much time. Moreover, the influence of New American Schools on ATLAS has tended to eclipse other influences. Indeed, the continuing relationship between ATLAS and New American Schools has had a significant impact on the current ATLAS theory of action. NAS has supported—both materially and in other ways—the evolution of ATLAS into a fee-for-service organization. Through its partnerships with various large jurisdictions, NAS also has supported ATLAS in its quest for client districts and schools. The interest of NAS in promoting designs that can be adopted by large numbers of schools also has influenced the size, roles, and responsibilities of the ATLAS staff. For example, NAS has provided some funding and consultation to help ATLAS and the other NAS design teams to streamline their organizations and to become more cost-effective.

FIVE SCHOOL REFORM ORGANIZATIONS
AND 108 YEARS OF EXPERIENCE

ATLAS did not achieve a grand synthesis encompassing all the moves, strategies, and principles of the four partner organizations or integrating their distinct theories of action. But ATLAS today has used the ideas and strategies of the four organizations as a jumping-off point. ATLAS has benefited from access to the people and resources of the four organizations and continuing conversations and interactions with Comer, Gardner, Sizer, and Whitla. However, the roots of ATLAS today stretch beyond the theories of action and the histories of the four partner organizations to draw on other organizations and individuals. Among the organizations are Accelerated Schools, with which Gerstle has been associated, and New American Schools and its other design teams. Among the individuals are Carlene Murphy and the other staff members who have joined ATLAS in recent years. Like its parent organizations in their early years, ATLAS is developing a theory of action as it goes along, one rooted in the backgrounds and personalities of the individuals most directly involved with it, affected by the diverse contexts in which it works, and reflecting the ideas of its time.

Throughout this book we have contrasted the theories of action of four school reform organizations, and in this chapter we have added a fifth. However, we have claimed throughout that in terms of what we think is most important, there is little to contrast. All five of the organizations discussed in this book work behind the scenes, where we think the real challenges are. They attempt to take into account the complexity of schools. They all work with schooling's insiders. They all respect the fact that change takes time.

Still, differences matter. Many of the differences that persist among the five ATLAS organizations are crucial to their identity and help animate their work. One lesson we take from the ATLAS story is that school reform programs cannot easily be mixed and matched, or reassembled to form new or greater wholes—that in this sense the quest for a grand design synthesis is futile.

On the other hand, school reform as practiced by these organizations is not about implementing programs. It is really about school communities rethinking their beliefs and values, and reconstructing their practices. In this sense, the grand design synthesis *is* achievable, but only within the context of each unique school community. That is the other important lesson of the ATLAS story—one that continues to unfold in the work of ATLAS, the Coalition of Essential Schools, the School Development Program, Education Development Center, and Project Zero. It has to do with the crucial help that such outside reformers bring to inside reformers as they struggle to create school designs that are different from the norm and uniquely their own.

Afterword

This volume tells the story of four quite different organizations joining together to create a new enterprise that would be a powerful synthesis of each group's prior work and history. As the principal investigators for this effort, we hope the reader will gain from this volume what we have gained from several years of exploring the meaning or our partnerships to create ATLAS: a much expanded view of the many valid but different starting points, strategies, and moves that organizations can adopt to reach the common goal of a good education for all our children. We use this afterword to put forth a few personal and philosophical comments that express our own, albeit biased, view of this joint endeavor.

In the introduction to this volume, the authors point out that together, our four organizations—the School Development Program (SDP), the Coalition of Essential Schools (CES), Education Development Center, and Harvard Project Zero (PZ)—represent more than 100 years of school reform. What we do not claim is "100 years of silence." We each claim a strong voice in the movement to bring schools from an outmoded industrial model no longer appropriate to the twenty-first century world into a set of flexible yet rigorous experiences that push our children to high intellectual achievement and strong character—no matter our differences, no matter our separate methods and means. What united us, what continues to unite us, in collegial friendship is the passion of our convictions. Each of us, and each of our organizations, care deeply about the work of school reform, have stayed the course for a significant part of the twentieth century, and have not compromised our values and beliefs simply to accommodate to the changing winds of politics or fashion. In the old-fashioned sense, our organizations, whether formally or loosely configured, linked to a university or free-standing, are comprised of people of character and strong conviction.

Strong conviction, however, has its down side. It can get in the way of working together and reaching consensus. We cannot deny that our four organizations in their ongoing history and work retain their original goals and intentions. The methodologies of each organization remain essentially intact, ranging from the academic research framework of Project Zero to the practitioner-driven school reformations of the Coalition of Essential Schools, to the orienting ideas of child psychology and development in the School Development Program, to the mediation of external agents and the importance of new knowledge fostered by various EDC projects. But philosophies and principles—both expressed and implicit— show the mark of the collaboration.

Beyond the creation of ATLAS itself, ATLAS events and experiences did leave a significant residual within each organization. For example, the CES group was moved substantially forward by the discussions on "education for understanding" that occupied many of the ATLAS development and seminar meetings. And we can see that the importance of child and adolescent development has also had resonance, largely in the way CES people talk about such issues as "personalization," a key ATLAS concept.

For SDP as an organization, participating in ATLAS allowed key staff to explore and confirm their growing sense that strengthening curriculum in SDP schools would be an important next step in the work of creating child-supportive educational environments.

Members of PZ learned about the limitations of working at one school at a time and about the pros and cons of larger scale reform efforts like CES and SDP. At the same time, the work with the other organizations in ATLAS prompted strategic alliances that were pursued in other projects and fostered the exchange both of ideas and talented personnel with the other ATLAS partners. These links, in turn, have informed PZ's work in many areas including assessment and adult development.

At EDC, where comprehensive school reform has been a driving motivation for many years, participating in ATLAS brought a clearer framework for involving parents and community in school improvement and for linking the health and well-being of young people to schooling's academic purposes and goals.

In Chapter 6, the four organizations are described as having had "a somewhat uneasy partnership." Disequilibrium, however, can have a very positive effect—it can force growth and learning. Such is the case here, and certainly for the four principal investigators. This volume tells a story of discovery and recovery. Through an examination of what makes each of us "tick" and gives impetus to our activities, we discovered that we do indeed have differences in the values we hold and the ways we choose to play our roles as instigators and partners in local school districts. But we learned that we also share an unshaken conviction that change and progress are possible, and a centering around the development and well-being of young people in the institutions we call "school." We helped each

other as a group, not simply as individuals, to express and thus keep un-
covering and recovering our founding principles and beliefs.

The important outcome of our partnering—an outcome not necessarily
anticipated nor well-conceived at the outset—is a new respect for our differences and willingness to let these differences co-exist in friendly har-
mony. Rather than continuing to strive for an end that was doomed to
failure, or total consensus around our methods and ways of working within
ATLAS, we began to see the value and power of our several ways of addressing similar challenges in the reform of schooling. By allowing our
diversity of styles to coexist and complement each other, we found our
pathway to an inclusive and still coherent framework for the ATLAS design that capitalized on the variety of strengths no one of us alone could
muster. We each found a niche. That's an important and worthwhile lesson, we believe, for all organizations to consider.

A few years ago, Margaret Wheatley and her colleague Myron Kellner-
Rogers wrote a deceptively simple book about organizational development
titled plainly, "A Simpler Way." They really captured what we "learned
by doing."

> Life creates niches not to dominate but to support. . . . Niches are an ex-
> ample of symbiosis. Niches are created when an individual or population
> defines itself. . . . This process of specializing in order to remain together is
> difficult for us to comprehend. We have explained the world of organizing
> so differently. We have looked for competition and used it to explain the
> behaviors that we see. . . . But living systems cannot be explained by com-
> petition. . . . The birds and the cacti and the bees adapt so that they can
> remain together. . . . They are using their differences to find new ways of
> living together. (pp. 42–43)

The authors of this volume argue that a "grand synthesis . . . a summing
up of one hundred years of diverse theories of action" was an "impossible
and an undesirable goal." From our point of view, however, ATLAS in its
essential elements represents, if not a total synthesis, at the very least a
well-integrated design with traceable lineage to each partner organization's
work. ATLAS has indeed provided the idea, practices and people of each
group with "new ways of living together." From our different home bases,
we came together to found a new community of "authentic teaching,
learning and assessment for all students." By acknowledging and participating in that community, we were each made more whole and more
capacious in our thinking about schools and our understanding of good
education. ATLAS is called the "fifth organization" by the authors; to the
four of us, it represents a natural extension of our individuality into a

collective enterprise that both complements and challenges each of its parents. It is indeed our child, and we are proud to be involved in preparing it for an independent life in the world of learning.

Janet Whitla, *Education Development Center*
James Comer, *School Development Program*
Howard Gardner, *Harvard Project Zero*
Theodore Sizer, *Coalition of Essential Schools*

Appendix

ATLAS COMMUNITIES
Education Development Center, Inc.
55 Chapel Street
Newton, MA 02158-1060
Phone: (617) 969-7100
FAX: (617) 969-3440
http://www.edc.org/FSC/ATLAS/

James Comer, Howard Gardner, Theodore Sizer,
and Janet Whitla, *Principal Investigators*
Linda Gerstle, *Director*

Selected publications

ATLAS Communities (1997). *Charting the course.* Newton, MA: Education Development Center.
Murphy, C. U., & Lick, D. W. (1998). *Whole faculty study groups.* Thousand Oaks, CA: Corwin Press.
To subscribe to an e-mail newsletter or for further information, contact: atlas@edc.org

COALITION OF ESSENTIAL SCHOOLS, NATIONAL OFFICE
1814 Franklin St., Suite 700
Oakland, CA 94612
Phone: (510) 433-1451
FAX: (510) 433-1455
http://www.essentialschools.org

Theodore Sizer, *Chairman*
Amy Gerstein, *Executive Director*

Selected publications

McDonald, J. P. (1996). *Redesigning school.* San Francisco: Jossey Bass.
Muncey, D. E., & McQuillan, P. J. (1996). *Reform and resistance in schools and classrooms: An ethnographic view of the coalition of essential schools.* New Haven: Yale University Press.
Sizer, T. R. (1984). *Horace's compromise: The dilemma of the American high school.* Boston: Houghton Mifflin.

Sizer, T. R. (1992). *Horace's school: Redesigning the American high school*. Boston: Houghton Mifflin.

Sizer, T. R. (1996). *Horace's hope: What works for the American high school*. Boston: Houghton Mifflin.

Wasley, P. A. (1995). *Stirring the chalkdust: Tales of teachers changing classroom practice*. New York: Teachers College Press.

Wasley, P., Hampel, R., & Clark, R. (1997). *Kids and school reform*. San Francisco: Jossey Bass.

To subscribe to *Horace*, the journal of the Coalition for Essential Schools, or for further information contact: Helen Ortiz (510) 433-1541.

EDUCATION DEVELOPMENT CENTER
55 Chapel Street
Newton, MA 02158-1060
Phone: (617) 969-7100
FAX: (617) 969-3440
http://www.edc.org

Janet Whitla, *President*

Selected Publications

Ames, N. & Miller, E. (1994) *Changing middle schools: How to make schools work for young adolescents*. San Francisco: Jossey-Bass.

Education Development Center. (1988). *Building ATLAS communities: Charting the course*. For information about EDC's most recent projects and publications send messages to: www@edc.org.

Education Development Center & National Science Foundation. (1997). *Foundations: The challenge and promise of K–8 science education reform*. Washington, D.C.: National Science Foundation.

Miller, B. & Kantrov, I. (Eds.) (1998). *Casebook on school reform*. Portsmouth, NH: Heinemann.

Schifter, D. & Fosnot, C. T. (1993). *Reconstructing mathematics education: Stories of teachers meeting the challenge of reform*. New York: Teachers College Press.

Zorfass, J. M. & Copel, H. (1998). *Teaching middle school students to be active researchers*. Alexandria, VA: Association for Supervision and Curriculum Development.

PROJECT ZERO
Longfellow Hall
Appian Way
Cambridge, MA 02138
Phone: (617) 495-4342
http://pzweb.harvard.edu/

Howard Gardner and David Perkins, *Co-Directors*

Selected publications

Blythe, T. (1997). *The teaching for understanding guide*. San Francisco: Jossey Bass.

Gardner, H. (1983). *Frames of mind*. New York: Basic Books.

Perkins, D. (1992). *Smart schools: From training memories to educating minds*. New York: The Free Press.

Seidel, S., Walters, J., Kirby, E., Olff, N., Powell, K., Scripp, L., & Veenema, S. (1997). *Portfolio practices: Thinking through the assessment of children's work*. Washington: NEA Professional Library Publication.

Wiske, M. S. (Ed.). (1997). *Teaching for understanding: Linking research with practice*. San Francisco: Jossey Bass.

If you wish to contact Project Zero, please send mail to: info@pz.harvard.edu

SCHOOL DEVELOPMENT PROGRAM
55 College Street
New Haven, CT 06510
Phone: (203) 737-1020
FAX: (203) 737-1023
http://info.med.yale.edu/comer/

James Comer, *Founder*
Edward Joyner, *Executive Director*

Selected publications

Comer, J. P. (1988). *Maggie's American dream*. New York: Penguin.

Comer, J. P. (1993). *School power: Implications of an intervention project*, Revised. New York: The Free Press.

Comer, J. P. (1997). *Waiting for a miracle: Why schools can't solve our problems—and how we can*. New York: Dutton.

Comer, J. P., Haynes, N. M., Joyner, E. T., & Ben-Avie, M. (1996). *Rallying the whole village: The Comer process for reforming education*. New York: Teachers College Press.

To subscribe to Newsline the newsletter of the School Development Program or for more information about the School Development Program, contact Joanne Corbin: joanne.corbin@yale.edu

Notes

CHAPTER 1

1. Although independent, NASDC was formed with the encouragement of President Bush and was later endorsed by President Clinton.

2. The four principals of the Atlas Seminar were James Comer, Howard Gardner, Theodore Sizer, and Janet Whitla. Most of the other members of the Seminar were also staff members of the four partner organizations, including ATLAS itself. Several school people were members too—associates of the three original ATLAS sites: Prince George's County, MD; Gorham, ME; and Norfolk, VA. Finally, there were several members of the Seminar who were invited to contribute their outside perspectives: Anthony Alvarado, Beverly Falk, Nathan Glazer, Edmund Gordon, Ann Lieberman, and Mary Metz.

3. EDC is headquartered in Newton, MA; PZ in Cambridge, MA; and SDP in New Haven, CT. In the summer of 1998, CES moved its national headquarters from Providence, RI, to Oakland, CA.

4. Some members of the Cognitive Skills Group at PZ participated in some ATLAS activities, however. For example, David Perkins was a member of the ATLAS Seminar. For this reason (and also simply for ease of exposition), we simply will use the term PZ in referring to the ATLAS partner, although the reader should know that we mean primarily the Development Group at PZ.

CHAPTER 2

1. In both the SDP and the CES theories of action, the school is the critical unit of reform. However, as a result of a number of factors discussed below, SDP puts far greater emphasis than CES on the district as a key partner in reform. In this sense, SDP membership—as distinct from CES—is much more likely to involve the district, often as the initiator of the relationship.

CHAPTER 5

1. Expeditionary Learning is a collaborative school reform effort, whose partners include Outward Bound and the Harvard Graduate School of Education. Its headquarters is at Harvard.

CHAPTER 6

1. In Schön's formulation, a theory of action is a "useful fiction" that struggles "to make itself come true" (Schön & McDonald, 1998). Thus the "holding" of a theory of action is actually an intermediate goal for the organization rather than a starting condition. The leaders of an initiative—aided by evaluators, according to Schön's theory of evaluation—struggle to define a theory of action and then struggle to hold onto it in the face of predictable and unpredictable threats from the environment.

2. Yet the Seminar launched the ethnography of ATLAS, which studied all facets: organization, seminar, and sites.

3. At the completion of the "Development Phase" of its work, NASDC shortened its name to New American Schools (NAS).

References

Argyris C., & Schön, D. A. (1992). *Theory in practice: Increasing professional effectiveness.* San Francisco: Jossey Bass. (Original work published 1974)

ATLAS Seminar. (1995). *Second-year report.* Providence, RI: Brown University.

Blythe, T. (1997). *The teaching for understanding guide.* San Francisco: Jossey Bass.

Bodilly, S. (1996). *Lessons from New American Schools Development Corporation's demonstration phase.* Santa Monica, CA: Rand.

Campbell, E. D. (1974). *Changing the direction of a non-profit organization.* Doctoral dissertation, Harvard Graduate School of Education, Cambridge, MA.

Coalition of Essential Schools. (1995, November). *Looking to the future: From conversation to demonstration* (Monograph). Providence, RI: Brown University.

Coalition of Essential Schools. (1996, August). *Profile of organizational structure* (Pamphlet). Providence, RI: Brown University.

Comer, J. P. (1980). *School power.* New York: Free Press.

Comer, J. P. (1994). *A brief history of the school development program.* Unpublished paper prepared for the School Development Program, Yale University, New Haven.

Comer, J. P. (1996). Comer: Waiting for a miracle. *SDP Newsline, 5* (1), pp. 1–8.

Comer, J. P., Haynes, N. M., Joyner, E. T., & Ben-Avie, M. (Eds.). (1996). *Rallying the whole village: The Comer process for reforming education.* New York: Teachers College Press.

Dow, P. B. (1991). *Schoolhouse politics: Lessons from the Sputnik era.* Cambridge, MA: Harvard University Press.

Duckworth, E. (1987). *"The having of wonderful ideas" and other essays on teaching and learning.* New York: Teachers College Press.

Evans, P. M. (1994). Getting beyond chewing gum and book covers. *Education Week, 14* (7), 44.

Fanning, K., Muncey, D., & White, N. (1994, September). *ATLAS Seminar ethnography project first year report.* Unpublished paper, Brown University, Providence, RI.

Gardner, H. (1983). *Frames of mind.* New York: Basic Books.

Gardner, H. (1993). *Multiple intelligences: The Theory in Practice.* New York: Basic Books.

Gardner, H. (1995). Reflections on multiple intelligences: Myths and messages. *Phi Delta Kappan, 77*(3), 200–209.

Gardner, H., & Boix-Mansilla, V. (1994). Teaching for understanding in the disciplines—and beyond. *Teachers College Record, 96*(2), 19–31.

Gillette, J. H., & Kranyik, R. D. (1996). Changing American schools: Insights from the School Development Program. In J. P. Comer, N. M. Haynes, E. T. Joyner, & M. Ben-Avie (Eds.), *Rallying the whole village: The Comer process for reforming education* (pp. 147–168). New York: Teachers College Press.

Hatch, T. (1998a). The differences in theory that matter in the practice of school improvement. *American Educational Research Journal, 35*(1), 3–32.

Hatch, T. (1998b). How comprehensive can comprehensive reform be? *Phi Delta Kappan, 79* (7), 518–523.

Hatch, T. (1998c). *What does it take to break the mold? Rhetoric and reality in New American Schools.* Unpublished paper. ATLAS Seminar. Providence, RI: Brown University.

Hatch, T., & White, N. (1997, July). *The raw materials of educational reform: Rethinking the knowledge of school improvement.* Unpublished paper, ATLAS Seminar. Brown University, Providence, RI.

Horton, M., Kohl, J., & Kohl, H. (1990). *The long haul: An autobiography.* New York: Anchor Books.

King, S., Louth, C., & Wasley P. (April, 1993). *Roses, retrievers, and research: Collaborative inquiry to foster better schools.* Paper presented at the annual meeting of the American Educational Research Association, Atlanta.

Krechevsky, M., & Morocco, C. (1996). *Professional development: Four propositions.* Paper prepared for the ATLAS Seminar, Harvard Graduate School of Education, Cambridge, MA.

Lear, R. (1993). *Developing valuable habits in ATLAS students.* ATLAS Communities Project, Providence, RI.

Leventhal, D., & March, J. (1993). The myopia of learning. *Strategic Management Journal, 14,* 95–112.

March, J. (1991). Exploration and exploitation in organizational learning. *Organization Science, 2*(1), 71–87.

McDonald, J. P. (1996). *Redesigning school.* San Francisco: Jossey Bass.

McDonald, J. P., Smith, S., Turner, D., Finney, M., & Barton, E. (1993). *Graduation by exhibition.* Alexandria, VA: Association for Supervision and Curriculum Development.

Muncey, D. E., & McQuillan, P. J. (1996). *Reform and resistance in schools and classrooms: An ethnographic view of the Coalition of Essential Schools.* New Haven: Yale University Press.

National Commission on Excellence in Education. (1983). *A nation at risk: The imperative for educational reform.* Washington, DC: U.S. Department of Education.

Powell, A., Farrar, E., & Cohen, D. K. (1985). *The shopping mall high school.* Boston: Houghton Mifflin.

Proposal to the New American Schools Development Corporation. (1991). ATLAS Communities Project, Providence, RI.

Rogers, B. (1996). *Four sources of authority for curriculum decisions.* ATLAS Seminar, Cambridge, MA.

Sarason, S. B. (1982). *The culture of the school and the problem of change* (2nd ed.). San Francisco: Jossey Bass.

Sarason, S. B. (1991). *The predictable failure of educational reform.* San Francisco: Jossey Bass.

Sarason, S. B. (1996). *Revisiting the culture of the school and the problem of change.* New York: Teachers College Press.

Schön, D. A. (1997, April). *Notes for a theory of action approach to evaluation.* Paper presented at a colloquium at the Harvard Graduate School of Education, Cambridge, MA.

Schön, D. A., & McDonald, J. P. (1998). *Doing what you mean to do in school reform* (Monograph). Providence, RI: Annenberg Institute, Brown University.

Schorr, L. B. (1988). *Within our reach: Breaking the cycle of disadvantage.* New York: Anchor Books/Doubleday.

Senge, P. (1990). *The fifth discipline: The art and practice of the learning organization.* New York: Doubleday.

Sizer, T. R. (1964). *Secondary schools at the turn of the century.* New Haven: Yale University Press.

Sizer, T. R. (1984). *Horace's compromise: The dilemma of the American high school.* Boston: Houghton Mifflin.

Sizer, T. R. (1992a). *Horace's school: Redesigning the American high school.* Boston: Houghton Mifflin.

Sizer, T. R. (1992b). Unpublished memo to the curriculum group of the ATLAS Seminar, Brown University, Providence, RI.

Sizer, T. R. (1996). *Horace's hope: What works for the American high school.* Boston: Houghton Mifflin.

Smith, D., & Kaltenbaugh, L. (1996). University–school partnership: Reforming teacher preparation. In J. P. Comer, N. M. Haynes, E. T. Joyner, & M. Ben-Avie (Eds.), *Rallying the whole village: The Comer process for reforming education* (pp. 72–97). New York: Teachers College Press.

Squires, D. A., & Joyner, E. T. (1996). Time and alignment: Potent tools for improving achievement. In J. P. Comer, N. M. Haynes, E. T. Joyner, & M. Ben-Avie (Eds.), *Rallying the whole village: The Comer process for reforming education* (pp. 98–122). New York: Teachers College Press.

Stringfield, S., & Herman, B. (1994). *Observations of partial implementations of the Coalition of Essential Schools: The need for higher reliability organizational methods.* Baltimore, MD: Johns Hopkins University, Center for Research on Effective Schooling for Disadvantaged Students.

Stringfield, S., Ross, S., & Smith, L. (Eds.). (1996). *Bold plans for school restructuring: The New American Schools Development Corporation designs.* Mahwah, NJ: Erlbaum.

Wahl, E. (1995, January 13). *The impact of EDC* (First Draft, Preliminary Report). Newton, MA: Education Development Center.

Wasley, P. A. (1995). *Stirring the chalkdust: Tales of teachers changing classroom practice.* New York: Teachers College Press.

Wasley, P. A., Hampel, R., & Clark, R. (1997a). *Kids and school reform.* San Francisco: Jossey Bass.

Wasley, P. A., Hampel, R., & Clark, R. (1997b). The puzzle of whole-school change. *Phi Delta Kappan, 78* (9), 690–697.

Wasley, P. A., King, S. P., & Louth, C. (1995). Creating coalition schools through collaborative inquiry. In J. Oakes & K. H. Quartz (Eds.), *Creating new educational communities: 94th NSSE Yearbook, Part I* (pp. 203–223). Chicago: National Society for the Study of Education, University of Chicago Press.

Wheatley, M. J. (1996). *A simpler way.* San Francisco: Berrett-Koehler.

White, N., Fanning, K., & Muncey, D. M. (1995, September 29). *ATLAS Seminar ethnography project third report: Exhibitions in the Gorham and Norfolk ATLAS pathways: 1994–95.* Unpublished report, Brown University, Providence, RI.

White, N., Muncey, D. M., & Fanning, K. (1998). ATLAS Seminar Ethnography Project Final Report. Providence, RI: Brown University.

Whitla, J. (1996). *The president's notebook.* Newton, MA: Education Development Center, Inc.

Wiske, M. S. (Ed.). (1997). *Teaching for understanding: Linking research with practice.* San Francisco: Jossey Bass.

About the Authors

Joseph P. McDonald is Professor of Teaching and Learning at New York University's School of Education. He teaches courses in teaching, curriculum, and educational policy to both undergraduates and graduate students. He also co-leads the cross-site evaluation of the billion-dollar-plus Annenberg Challenge. Dr. McDonald was a high school teacher for 17 years, and was also a high school principal. For many years he taught at Brown University, where he was also a senior researcher at the Coalition of Essential Schools and the first Director of Research at the Annenberg Institute. He is the author of *Redesigning School* (Jossey-Bass, 1996), *Teaching: Making Sense of an Uncertain Craft* (Teachers College Press, 1992), and editor and co-author of *Graduation by Exhibition: Assessing Genuine Achievement* (ASCD, 1993).

Thomas Hatch is a Senior Scholar at The Carnegie Foundation for the Advancement of Teaching. His research focuses on normal and exceptional development and the contexts and conditions that support them. Currently, he serves as a co-director of the program for K–12 teachers and teacher educators of the Carnegie Academy for the Scholarship of Teaching and Learning and leads projects exploring the opportunities and obstacles of school reform. Before joining the Carnegie Foundation, he spent 12 years at Harvard Project Zero. During that time, he was a participant in the ATLAS Project and Director of the ATLAS Seminar.

Edward Kirby is the Director of Charter School Accountability for the Massachusetts Department of Education. He is responsible for overseeing and evaluating the academic and organizational performance of the state's 34 public charter schools. The accountability process which he manages produces recommendations to the Massachusetts Board of Education to renew or revoke each school's charter every five years. Before joining the Department's Charter School Office, he worked as a consulting analyst and writer to studies of education policy and school reform. He began work in education as a high school English teacher and track/cross-country coach.

143

Nancy Ames is Vice President of Education Development Center, Inc. and Director of the Center for Family, School, and Community. She is co-author of *Changing Middle Schools* (Jossey-Bass, 1994), which highlighted four urban middle schools that underwent deep transformation. She currently coordinates the *National Forum to Accelerate Middle-Grades Reform*, which brings together 40 education leaders to develop a shared vision and an integrated plan of action. In addition to her work in middle level education, Ms. Ames has more than 30 years of experience in education research and evaluation, policy and program development, and technical assistance. Her work spans all levels of the educational system—state, district, school, and classroom—and encompasses all aspects of systemic reform, including state and local policy, standards and assessment, school restructuring, professional development, and parent/community involvement.

Norris M. Haynes is Professor in the Counseling and School Psychology Department at Southern Connecticut State University and Director of the Center for School Action Research and Improvement. He is also Associate Clinical Professor of Psychology, Education and Child Development at the Yale Child Study Center. He is also a member of the faculty in the Yale Department of Psychology and the Bush Center. Dr. Haynes served as director of research for the Comer School Development Program (SDP) from 1985–1998 and contributes significantly to the SDP's training and dissemination activities. He was responsible for designing the dissemination plan and for developing and preparing grant applications in support of the SDP's national dissemination strategies.

Dr. Haynes earned a B.A. in Psychology and Master of Science and Advanced Certificate in Education and Counseling Psychology from the State University of New York. He earned a Ph.D. in Educational Psychology from Howard University in 1978. He also holds a Master's Business Administration with a concentration in Public Health and Health Services Administration. He completed a two-year Mid-Career Post Doctoral Fellowship in Psychology at Yale University.

Dr. Haynes has taught at the elementary and high school levels. He has been a professor at Howard University and adjunct professor at several other universities. He is the author and co-author of many articles, book chapters and books. His books include: *Critical Issues in Educating African-American Children*; *Promoting Social and Emotional Learning: Guidelines for Educators*; and *Rallying the Whole Village: The Comer Process for Reforming Education*. He is also the co-author of books which are in press, including: *Promoting Motivation, Learning and Achievement Among Urban Middle and High School Students* and *Child by Child, Adult by Adult and School by School*.

Edward T. Joyner is the Executive Director of the School Development Program at the Yale Child Study Center. He received a B.A. in Social Science from Elizabeth City State University in North Carolina and a M.A.T. from Wesleyan University in 1973. He received an Ed.D. in Educational Administration from the University of Bridgeport in 1989.

Dr. Joyner has taught at both the high school and college levels. He served as an assistant principal at Hillhouse High School and principal of Jackie Robinson Middle School in New Haven, Connecticut. He has published articles dealing with at-risk youth, and for local school districts has developed training manuals related to school change as a response to changing student and community needs. Dr. Joyner is married to Shirley Love Joyner, a guidance counselor with the New Haven Public Schools in Connecticut. Together they have two children, Monica Joyner, a teacher in the Prince George's County Public Schools in Maryland, and Edward Joyner, Jr., a sophomore college student.

Index